Discovery Science

Explorations for the Early Years

Grade Pre-Kindergarten

David A. Winnett

Robert E. Rockwell

Elizabeth A. Sherwood

Robert A. Williams

Innovative Learning Publications

Addison-Wesley Publishing Company
Menlo Park, California • Reading, Massachusetts • New York
Don Mills, Ontario • Wokingham, England • Amsterdam
Bonn • Milan • Madrid • Sydney • Singapore • Tokyo
Seoul • Taipei • Mexico City • San Juan

Lela DeToye served as a contributing author and language arts consultant.

Project Editor: *Mali Apple*
Production Coordinator: *Claire Flaherty*
Design Manager: *Jeff Kelly*
Cover and Text Design: *Christy Butterfield*
Photographs: *Bill Brinson*
Illustrations: *Rachel Gage*
Composition: *Andrea Reider*

This book is published by Innovative Learning Publications™, an imprint of the Alternative Publishing Group of Addison-Wesley Publishing Company.

ISBN 0-201-49364-0

5 6 7 8 9 10-ML-03 02 01 00

This Book Is Printed
on Recycled Paper

Acknowledgments

The authors of Discovery Science would like to offer a sincere thank you to the Discovery Science Project Staff: Ann Scates, Coordinator; Lela DeToye, Language Consultant; and Sharon Winnett, Language and Early Childhood Specialist.

We'd also like to thank Early Childhood Specialists Debbi Keilor, Anne Huber, Debbie Noyes, Angela Karban, and Debby Rahm; and Mali Apple, our editor, for the pride and commitment she has given to Discovery Science.

We also want to express our sincere appreciation to the children, teachers, administrators, and families of the many early childhood programs that provided assistance and direction in the development of this curriculum: Collinsville Prekindergarten, Collinsville Unit 10, Collinsville, Ill.; Hillsboro Prekindergarten Program, Hillsboro Community Unit School District #3, Hillsboro, Ill.; Bright Horizons Conservatoire, Carrollton, Tex.; FSVNA–Madison County Head Start: Alton, Granite City, Pontoon Beach, Venice, Edwardsville, and Collinsville, Ill.; Southern Illinois University Early Childhood Center, Edwardsville, Ill.; Discovery School, O'Fallon, Ill.; and Tree Hut Preschool and Childcare Center, Belleville, Ill.

Dedication

To my mother, Jacqueline, and my father, David R. You started my life with love and tender emotions that only come from loving parents. I am so blessed that you are both here today to share in the rewards of your forty-five years of effort and hard work.
D. A. W.

To my mother, Erma Lee, who made all things possible. To my wife, Donna, for her love and constant support throughout this project. To my daughters, Janet and Susan, for their continued encouragement and acceptance. To my grandchildren, Teri, Robert, Amanda, Michael, and Kathryn, for their wonder and willingness to try their grandpa's experiments. I love you all.
R. E. R.

To my friends—the Collinsville Pre-Kindergarten staff. You have given me support, encouragement, and inspiration. You have become my family: Cathy and Linda, Laura and Sandy, Kathy and Gloria, Margie and Michelle, Mary Beth and Jenna, Pam and Jan, Margo, Dennis, and, of course, Glenna. To my children—my prime motivators—Jennifer and Will.
E. A. S.

To the Earth: May it remain healthy and provide a safe home for all the children who will use the skills garnered from these activities. And to my mother, Katie: You are special.
R. A. W.

CONTENTS

UNIT 2: HOW OBJECTS MOVE   105

UNIT 3: HOW OBJECTS CHANGE 161

SAND AND WATER CENTER

DISCOVERY CENTER

SMALL GROUP

GOING OUTDOORS

UNIT 4: HOW OBJECTS ARE MADE AND USED

LANGUAGE AND READING CENTER 230

ART CENTER

AN INTRODUCTION TO DISCOVERY SCIENCE

What Is Discovery Science?

Discovery Science exposes children to much more than science skills and concepts. It gives children the opportunity to explore, experiment, create, and problem solve. It encourages them to refine their use of language as they talk about what they do or explain what they have discovered. It allows them to apply their emerging mathematical skills in the meaningful context of discovery. Discovery Science provides teachers with a curricular framework that capitalizes on the spirit of excitement for discovery that dwells in the minds of children, young and old.

What Is the Focus of Science for Young Children?

Discovery Science visualizes children as learners actively constructing knowledge rather than passively taking in information. Through their individual activity, children form knowledge and make it their own. They come to the educational setting with diverse backgrounds and experiences. It is essential that science, mathematics, and literacy skills be part of an integrated curriculum that recognizes and builds from this diversity.

The goals that follow are the foundation for building a successful early childhood science learning system—a system cognizant that the ultimate responsibility for learning lies with the learner; a system allowing that each learner is different and unique; a system enabling children to fulfill Jean Piaget's goal of education: "To create people who are capable of doing new things, not simply repeating what other generations have done—people who are creative inventors and discoverers."

Goals for Early Childhood Science

1. To provide an environment that supports active discovery

2. To promote the development of fundamental problem-solving skills

3. To promote personality dispositions indicative of good scientific problem solvers

4. To promote children's awareness of careers in science, mathematics, and technology

5. To raise children's comfort and confidence level with science through conscious efforts to counter bias against science

6. To promote development of a knowledge base of basic scientific principles and laws, providing the foundation upon which a clear and accurate understanding of the world can develop. A solid foundation reduces the risk of children acquiring misconceptions that may hinder later their understanding of more complex science concepts

Why Is Empowerment So Important?

We define empowerment as follows: To allow a person the sense of power to make decisions and to take actions on one's own volition. The inquiry model that prevails in Discovery Science is based on a foundation that begins with asking the children: What do you know? This is followed by Free Discovery, in which children explore materials on their own. Then the children are asked: What did you learn? This question is followed by experiences developed and structured for children to ask questions and to seek their own answers. Children are *empowered* to become scientists.

This sense of empowerment frees children to inquire, to explore, and to seek information and answers based on their own natural curiosity. They should be able to see science as a way to investigate the world and realize that science is all around them. Because children are natural inventors, they take delight in thinking, making, and doing. As they begin Free Discovery, they are taking the first steps toward the development of technological ability. Making and doing requires them to raise questions, thus building the structural base for later scientific thinking.

Why Is the Curriculum Built Around a Limited Number of Science Themes?

Often activity guides for young children contain a scattered collection of science concepts and terms that children are expected to absorb during their brief time as preschoolers. A hurried exposure to science may fail to provide the opportunity for the rich conceptual development that is possible with a more coherent, thoughtful approach. In keeping with the guidelines of Project 2061, Discovery Science works with only three basic science process skills over two years. This enables children ages three and four to be totally immersed in the science processes that are within their developmental capabilities. When learning is centered around a small number of core concepts, the learner can spend enough time with the materials and concepts to master them.

Let's look at adult learners. Fred and Maria have enrolled in a craft class. In the first session they are introduced to working with stained glass, and they practice cutting glass and learn to connect the pieces. They come to the second session ready to learn more. Instead they are told that the class is moving on to ceramics. They learn a little about ceramics and are excited about creating something new. They come to the third session ready to continue with ceramics. The clay is gone. It has been replaced with equipment for wood carving. Instead of acquiring skills, Fred and Maria are acquiring frustration.

Too often, this is what we do to children. Instead of giving them the self-confidence that comes with mastering new ideas or skills, we move them quickly from one topic to the next. We are subtly teaching them to be satisfied with incompetence. With a limited number of topics, children have more opportunities to experience feelings of competence and mastery.

Our philosophy is that it is better to help children acquire a real understanding of a few concepts than to give them fragments of many topics. Materials should be accessible and the curriculum developed in such a way that children can return to or repeat experiences that they may have completed some time ago. Repetition reinforces children's awareness of their own competence and the confidence that awareness brings.

Discovery Science for preschool children provides many approaches for developing their understanding the science processes of Focused Observation, Observing to Classify, and the beginnings of Organizing and Communicating Observations. The curriculum employs the common areas of the preschool environment to initiate exposure to the appropriate science process skills. Through explorations in the centers—the Art Center, the Block Center, the Dramatic Play Center, the Language and Reading Center, the Sand and Water Center, the Discovery Center, and Going Outdoors (Nature's center)—the children are given many opportunities to observe, classify, and communicate. These skills are supported by your questions to and your observations of the children as they work.

As you work with the four units in *Discovery Science,* you will continue to use all areas of the classroom, as well as the outdoors. The Going Outdoors activities can be used throughout the year with both threes and fours. The activities are appropriate for the various seasons and sensitive to the diversity of environments available to preschool teachers.

Since this curriculum is designed for both three- and four-year-old children, you, as the teacher, must make some decisions as to how to best implement the program in your classroom. Some of you teach only threes or fours, others have multi-aged groupings. You will find the curriculum responsive to the needs of the children you serve.

How Does Discovery Science Support Emerging Language and Literacy Skills?

During the preschool years, children's language becomes increasingly complex. This is the time of questions. "Whys" are constant. It is a time when you must learn to listen carefully and answer the question being asked (not the one you think should be answered) or provide the means for the child to answer it.

Descriptive Language

Descriptive language is an emerging skill with preschoolers and needs adult support. Encourage the use of all the senses and help the children find words to describe what they perceive. At group time, talk about shared experiences, what the children saw and heard. Model descriptive language as you hold a gerbil, look at a snail in a magnifying box, or play and pour at the water table. Wonder "what if" with the children. Verbalize your own questions: "I wonder if hamsters like bananas?" "How could we find out if fish can hear?"

Comparative Language

Children at this age are just beginning to understand relationship terms such as *big* and *bigger, heavy* and *light, long* and *longer.* Use comparative language frequently as you work with the children. Science experiences provide many opportunities as you and the children investigate, explore and discover together. The children are also learning about opposites, such as *long* and *short* and *empty* and *full.* As they make observations, encourage comparison and classification of what they discover.

Three Types of Language Development

We are concerned with three types of language development in Discovery Science: receptive, expressive, and semantics. *Receptive language* consists of understanding words as they are spoken to the listener. *Expressive language* consists of the words we use to communicate. Such language develops as children are exposed to language in their environment. As teachers we use the words that we want children to learn and label items for children as we talk about them.

The most important stage of language development is *semantics.* This means that a person understands the meaning of a word and can use it appropriately. Listen to children as they talk with you and each other to learn whether they have a real understanding of the words they are using. Children grow in their understanding of new words through both hearing and using them. Model language, describe what you see them doing, and participate in *their* conversations to promote their development.

Discovery Science provides many opportunities for working with language and literacy. Language is a vital means by which concepts are explored and developed. As children share ideas and observations with each other both verbally and symbolically, they will be using a variety of language skills.

As educators we should allow children to share what they know in whatever way they can and to use that sharing as an opportunity to enhance communication skills. In this context Discovery Science will

- improve effective use and expansion of vocabulary as children seek to describe accurately their observations and to share their discoveries

- allow children to devise their own ways of communicating their experiences

- include group experiences that will model diverse uses of language and literacy

- familiarize children with the process of asking a question and looking for an answer, a process often confusing to young children

- introduce alternative methods of communication, such as demonstrations, drawings, charts, and dictated labels

- focus on effective communication and interesting and accurate content rather than precise grammar

- encourage sharing and collaboration, which both require meaningful communication

Discovery Charts

Discovery Charts offer the opportunity to reinforce the children's beginning understanding of the relationship between spoken language and the written word. They begin to realize that writing is talk put on paper. The development of Discovery Charts follows the progression of the book. The first section of each unit is open exploration and expansion of ideas throughout the classroom centers. The Discovery Charts should be open-ended and very simple.

For example, a Discovery Chart might be titled *What can you tell us about things that move?* or *How do you move a ball, a block, or your body?* Entries on the chart may be things such as:

LaMont: I push the button on the car and it moves really fast.

Abby: I can run faster.

Tisha: I can run faster, too.

As you work with the children, reread the Discovery Charts frequently. This helps the children understand the permanent nature of written language—that the same Discovery Chart says the same thing each time you read it. It also tells them that you value their language and that the work they do is important enough to write about and remember.

Discovery Books

Discovery Books are a key component of Discovery Science. They document the children's explorations, serve as a means of communicating with others, and support emerging literacy skills. It is a rewarding experience for children to review the books, see their own entries, and remind themselves of the things they have done. The books are also a permanent record of what they have learned that they can share with their families.

Make separate class Discovery Books for each unit. You can also center them around individual activities. The simplest way to make a Discovery Book is to staple several sheets of blank paper between two sheets of construction paper. Have children decorate the covers. To make the books sturdier for use in the class library area, it is best to laminate the covers or cover them with clear contact paper.

The class may want to publish a book on one of the content areas. Classes may want to borrow each other's books to compare findings. Photographs or videotapes may be used to document experiences, and children can provide captions or narrative.

Science Vocabulary

The Science Vocabulary in each activity is the specialized vocabulary that children need to understand semantically to fully understand the science concepts they are exploring. At this age, the words seem simple; however, understanding concepts such as *heavy* and *light* or how we define the word *animal* are quite new. We encourage you to work with the children to develop a broader understanding of the introduced words. This idea of seeking a more complete understanding of word meaning encourages children to use language freely.

We are trying to give children the confidence to explore and discover on their own—to have power over the direction their inquiry may follow. Misconceptions are corrected through additional experiences rather than through verbal correction of their understanding of the words.

What Is the Math Connection?

Science and mathematics fit together in a natural and very functional way. Mathematics is an essential component of communication for scientists. It also provides an effective way for children to process and share their discoveries.

Preschoolers are developing a beginning understanding of one-to-one correspondence and counting with purpose. They can use their hands or a double-pan balance to compare mass. Discovery Science provides many opportunities to work with an array of concepts such as more/less, alike/different, size relationships and seriation, matching, and classifying.

Rather than teaching these concepts and others in isolation, Discovery Science gives children the chance to gain science and mathematical knowledge together as part of a unified curriculum. The practical experience of connecting mathematical concepts with science experiences enables young children to begin to operationalize mathematical skills—increasing the chance that they will understand and appreciate mathematics as they grow and learn.

How Does Discovery Science Involve the Larger Community?

The introduction to each unit contains ideas for involving the community to expand the children's understanding of the science concepts being explored. Parents and other adults should be invited into the classroom to share hobbies and occupations relevant to the unit. A parent who likes to cook could make something with the children and talk about the changes occurring. An X-ray technician could bring in X rays of a broken bone and a healed bone. For the How Objects Are Alike and Different unit, you might find someone with a shell collection to share.

Field trips can support the children's learning. Take a trip to the grocery store and talk about how the fruits and vegetables are alike and different. Go to a car wash and watch how a car is *changed* from dirty to clean. Go to a fast-food restaurant and talk about the *tools* used to prepare food. Parents are a wonderful resource both for planning visits and field trips. Tell them your unit topics and some start-up ideas, and encourage their support.

What Is Free Discovery?

Children have a need to know. This natural curiosity, a fundamental drive to inquire, is as much a part of life as is breathing and eating. Free Discovery is observation and exploration at the children's own pace, a means to support their curiosity about the natural and physical environment in which they live. Having the freedom to explore at their own rate, without the fear of getting the "wrong" answers, is critical. In a secure and comfortable environment, children are able to fulfill their natural eagerness to find possible solutions to their own inquiries of why, what, how, and when in their own way. To accomplish this, Free Discovery should

- allow children to become familiar with the materials
- allow children to make observations and discoveries on their own and to feel good about them
- build children's self-esteem through their being in control of their own actions
- provide no right or wrong answers, and therefore no failure
- provide a nonthreatening learning time
- proceed at each child's own learning pace

The Role of Free Discovery

To be most effective, a science program must emphasize interaction with the environment, both natural and social. Using simple equipment and materials, children are given unlimited opportunities to explore and interact in their own ways. There are no set parameters within the limits of acceptable behavior. Exploratory freedom reigns. This can be a difficult time for adults, as we often want to step in at this phase of learning, intercepting children's natural and spontaneous curiosity with questions and challenges that are adult- rather than child-initiated. Children are often not ready for such interruptions. This phase of learning is the time to play with and explore materials in their own way. Free exploration and play are a need that must be fulfilled before children can see the materials as learning resources.

The idea of Free Discovery is inherent to good science, good teaching, and effective learning—for adults as well as children. As adults we simply have learned to complete this process more quickly than children because of our experience and knowledge base. How do we as adults approach learning a new skill?

Suppose that you would like to make a table but never have done any woodworking. Do you go buy some wood and some tools and get to work? No, you begin with Free Discovery. You may ask for some help from someone who has a bit more experience.

Maybe you will borrow a book or two and read about wood-working. You practice with the tools on wood scraps, not prime walnut. The more you work and the more you practice, the better you expect to perform. The surer you become of your skills, the more you are able to experiment and modify your techniques. With persistence you eventually learn enough to build the table you want. This slow flow of learning—moving from inexperience to experience to modification—is a natural process for the adult learner. It is also how children learn when they are given the opportunity.

In Free Discovery and in the Discovery Science activities that follow, the teacher and the children have specific roles.

The Role of the Teacher

- To encourage children to explore and to experiment independently
- To create an atmosphere conducive to learning
- To introduce new ideas, materials, and procedures
- To encourage inquiry and creativity
- To model inquiry, questioning, and problem solving
- To model safe practice
- To provide sufficient materials, information, and space for learning
- To support developmentally appropriate activity
- To assess and evaluate children's learning

The Role of the Children

- To care for themselves and function independently
- To understand that they are in control of their actions
- To feel good about discovery
- To cooperate with other children
- To collect data and document activities
- To explore with materials and ideas
- To realize that answers are not right or wrong but simply the results of inquiry
- To communicate about their experiences

How Do I Help Children Focus Their Observations?

Focused Observation activities allow teacher-directed quality control over the types of observations that children are making. Children are recording these observations in their minds. Later they can call up an observation and fit it into a larger conceptual framework that allows them to make sense of what they are doing or learning.

Because children will use the observations they make now as a basis on which to build future understanding, you have two major instructional concerns. First, there are observations about each of the four science themes that children need to make. If these observations are not made, children will not begin to understand the concepts. Second, children are continually making inferences about what they have observed. Some of these inferences are correct, and some may not be.

Focused Observation activities are designed to focus children's observations on specific aspects of each concept. Frequently you will ask the children to organize their observations to make them more precise. They will be asked to isolate various factors that affect their subject and to alter them to make new observations regarding the effect these changes have. For example, if you are rolling a ball down an inclined plane, what happens when you change the angle?

Children will become increasingly familiar with the process of making observations. You will become aware of their increasing ability to notice details and ask relevant questions. You will be able to assess their understanding of science concepts through the class Discovery Books, discussion, and your own observations.

How Do Children Observe to Classify?

Classification is an important skill for children to develop. Young learners naturally want to group and organize objects, and you probably will observe children classifying prior to these activities.

The simplest form of classification takes place when children start to collect similar objects and materials and assemble them together. Encourage this behavior by asking children to verbalize: Why are you putting all of these objects in the same place? Children's responses will likely indicate that a certain attribute has been identified and that the selections are based on that attribute. These children are well on their way to becoming skilled classifiers and will learn additional classification skills quickly. Children who are not displaying the initial desire to group and organize must be given special attention.

The Observing to Classify activities for each unit direct learners to develop increasingly more sophisticated skills. The initial activities ask children to repeat what they have probably been doing on their own: grouping objects according to a single attribute or a single physical property. To increase the difficulty level of the classification scheme, you later ask children to rank-order objects according to an increase or decrease in the magnitude of a specific property (for example, height, mass, or length).

Eventually you ask children to divide a group of objects by a particular attribute and then to further separate them into groups based on a second attribute. This final classification requires a child to hold two concepts in mind. For example, in the Unit 1 Going Outdoors section, the lesson Pull a Weed has children divide a group of plants according to type of root, either tap or diffused. Then the learners might separate these two groups according to size, those with larger diffused roots and those with smaller diffused roots.

Encouraging children to make use of their observations reinforces the importance of becoming good observers. Classification provides children with an opportunity to make decisions and to be in control. A successfully organized group of objects provides them immediate satisfaction in knowing that the task is over and is done well, similar to the feeling adults experience when all of the pieces of a puzzle fit together.

How Do I Help Children Organize and Communicate Observations?

Science seeks to find order and structure in our world. Free Discovery, Focused Observations, and Observations to Classify are the initial skills that young children need to begin establishing order in their world. Your task is to encourage children to describe their observations to the best of their ability. You will assist by asking questions, providing vocabulary, and urging the children to "tell more" or to show you what they know. At this age, children often understand more than they are able to verbalize. Be open to other kinds of communication. The words will come in time.

How Does Discovery Science Involve Families?

Families and early childhood educators need to work with each other because they have a common goal: concern for children. The home and the preschool are important functional areas for the young child. To assist the child and to provide the most effective learning environment, the preschool and the home must pull together to benefit the child. The early childhood Discovery Science program provides a natural avenue for children, families, and teachers to work together. A researcher (G. Thomas, "Cultivating the interest of women and minorities in high school mathematics," *Science Education* 70 (1986): 31–34) conducted a study of college students regarding their parents' involvement with their science education. The results revealed that positive family attitudes and encouragement were significant factors in fostering the students' interest in math and science. There was also a strong relationship in the extent to which these students enjoyed working on science hobbies as children and their science achievement in high school.

The Role of the Family

- To encourage discovery by the children
- To model inquiry and problem solving
- To resist answering and solving discovery activities before the child has done so
- To enjoy doing science activities with the child
- To feel free to communicate with the child's teacher, to ask questions, and to seek additional information when needed
- To listen to and give information to the child, always remembering that it is all right for any participant to make mistakes or to say "I don't know"
- To willingly share available resources from home, such as junk materials for making things or information and materials related to occupations or hobbies that correspond to the Discovery Science units

Family Connection Activities

There are two Family Connection activities for each unit, simple activities for the children to do at home with their families. Family Connection activities do not introduce new concepts; they reinforce what the children are learning at school. They empower children by giving them the opportunity to share their knowledge and expertise with their families.

The activities include a set of directions and a list of materials (often one or two items). Put the items and directions into a resealable plastic bag as a mini-kit for each child to take home.

Additional Ideas for Family Involvement

Introducing Discovery Science: A Family Meeting

This hands-on meeting invites families to be a part of Discovery Science. You will talk with families about the program and how it will be implemented. The family will interact with the Discovery Science activities and materials in the same way that their children will. After attending the meeting, families will be more adept at supporting, modeling, and discussing Discovery Science with their children.

The major focus of this meeting is to inform the parents of the strong emphasis that the Discovery Science curriculum places upon working with parents as partners in the education of their children. This meeting is designed to introduce the Family Connection activities and to let the families participate in assembling the mini-kits that will eventually be coming home with their children.

Plans for both family meetings, including sample invitations, fliers, planning checklists, sample meeting formats and evaluations are in the Family Connection section at the back of this book.

Discovery Science Newsletter

A Discovery Science newsletter can be a separate newsletter or simply a portion of a general newsletter designed to keep families informed of science-related activities at school and in the community. One page is enough to inform families of field trips, new animal visitors, or great discoveries that will help keep interest and input coming.

Family Letters

Send a letter home to families at the start of each Discovery Science unit to introduce the topic and to ask for support and ideas for resources. Sample letters are included in the Family Connection section.

Science-O-Grams: Discovery Notes

Brief notes can update families on current activities, remind them of an upcoming field trip or event, or tell them about their child's recent discovery.

Family Volunteers

Discovery Science can provide opportunities and access for families to volunteer both at school and at home. Family volunteers can enrich the learning process and expand the learning environment for children as they share their skills, personal expertise, and the enthusiasm of discovery.

THE CLASSROOM CENTERS

The children's play throughout the classroom provides a myriad of opportunities for exploring science concepts and gaining information. Science with young children can and should be done in almost any setting, just as science and its applications permeate the lives of adults.

The classroom centers, by their very nature, promote problem solving and positive risk taking because children work largely on their own. They learn to make independent decisions as they explore concepts designed to teach the how-to of science rather than words and facts. The classroom centers

- belong to all the children.
- provide ample materials in an accessible way.
- serve as a resource and library.
- provide safe and orderly places to work.
- set the stage and mood for exploration.

Setting Up the Classroom Centers: Storage and Management

Storage space must be thoughtfully designed to meet each classroom's instructional needs. Several types of storage are necessary. Some materials, such as magnifiers, paper, and a balance, should be out and available at all times, promoting their use and encouraging children to find new functions for them. Shelves, tables, and pegboard are useful for this type of storage.

Some materials must be stored out of the way until needed. Our experience with storage needs has led us to depend on plastic storage tubs, which are sold in local discount stores. They have lids, come in a variety of sizes, and stack easily, allowing whole sets of materials to be stored together. The availability of clear lids and a variety of colors increases their flexibility. The tubs can be made available to children or stored out of reach.

Other materials must be available but not necessarily set out on shelves. Resealable plastic bags are useful for holding small sets of materials. Small tubs, boxes, and crates are also helpful.

Regardless of the size and shape of your storage space and containers, they should be easy to clean and label, inexpensive, and easy for children to use and keep in order. Labeled shelves, racks, hooks, and storage closets can help. Also consider the following:

- Clutter-free surfaces for work areas.
- Places on shelves, tables, or the floor to leave materials for an extended time or study.
- Areas should be easy to clean. Cleanup materials should be readily available. Responsibility for accidents, along with normal messes, is part of science training.
- Children need plenty of freedom, time, equipment, and materials—properly cared for and stored in areas accessible to them—to become thoroughly involved.

Caring for Materials

The equipment and materials used in Discovery Science have been selected with young children in mind. For the most part, they are sturdy, durable, and require the same care as other classroom materials. Special care or storage requirements will be described when such materials are introduced. This information should be shared with the children.

Maintaining Safe Centers

The materials used in Discovery Science were chosen because they are inherently safe. We want the children who use these materials to be safe and to develop good safety habits. Safety and learning in the science area begun in the early years can lead to accident-free experiences later in school. A level of comfort with science makes careers in science and related occupations a more likely choice. To establish a safe science area:

- Model appropriate and safe behavior.
- Provide a safe place for children to work.
- Provide a way for children to work without overcrowding.
- Provide the special information necessary when equipment, materials, or situations might cause a problem.

Safety rules for classroom centers must be few, simple, and easy to follow. Well-planned and managed centers make this possible. Discuss safety rules each time a new material is introduced. Set clear limits regarding appropriate and inappropriate behavior to enable children to handle and interact with the materials safely. Your concern for safety, however, should be moderated by your good sense and control. Children must be protected, but they also need the chance to try things out.

The Language and Reading Center

Before you begin each unit, visit the library to select appropriate books. Discovery Science encourages experiences with real things, but you cannot bring the entire world into the classroom. Children will learn to expand their knowledge through the use of resource materials. A number of books appropriate for this age level are listed in each unit. Some of the books deal directly with science concepts. Many, however, have a much broader context. For example, *Hats, Hats, Hats,* by Ann Morris, which shows hats from around the world, provides an opportunity to reinforce concepts explored in How Objects Are Alike and Different. Many books with text that is too complex for this age will have illustrations the children will find interesting.

Posters and tapes will also add interest to the area. Display Discovery Books, Discovery Charts, and other examples of the children's work in the Language and Reading Center. The classroom environment becomes a more powerful place for children's learning when it has been enriched with books, magazines, posters, bulletin boards, pictures, card sets, and games. And it allows you to expose children to things you cannot bring into the classroom.

The Art Center

The Art Center provides material for self-expression, development of fine-motor skills, eye-hand coordination, and creativity along with the opportunity to explore, experiment, plan, and discover. As they work, children discover what the various materials can do, their physical characteristics, and how they can be manipulated in both predictable and unpredictable ways. When you introduce new materials, show the children how to care for them. This will result in a longer survival rate for the materials and will free the children to use them effectively.

In the early stages of work with any new material, the children's focus is clearly on manipulation, sensory exploration, and the process of gaining mastery and control. When children first begin to easel paint, their main interest is putting paint on paper. Many children will repeatedly cover the entire paper with paint. Other children will paint some lines and shapes and then cover them with another layer of paint. They are enjoying the feel of the brush on the paper, the process, with little if any focus on the finished product.

As they become comfortable with the materials, children are self-motivated to plan for a given outcome. Their work becomes more refined and organized. If allowed the freedom to work with various media in self-directed ways, children will begin to use increasingly complex and sophisticated processes. When you introduce new materials and techniques, children will approach them with curiosity and creativity.

As the children work with the variety of materials available in the Art Center, they are learning about

- *Focusing Observations.* Children use their senses to explore, experiment, and discover a diversity of textures, visual properties, and other characteristics of materials available to them.

- *Observing to Classify.* Children learn about the function and the use of media and equipment.

- *Organizing and Communicating Observations.* Children work together and share their experiences with you and the other children and dictate labels or stories about their creations.

- *Balance and Stability.* Children work with three-dimensional materials to create structures.

- *Spatial Relationships.* Children create collages, structures, or weavings and choose where to place paint or crayons on paper.

- *Physical Properties of Materials.* Children discover the many possibilities various media have to offer.

Give children ample opportunity to explore materials thoroughly. They need the experience of working with materials repeatedly to gain the sense of mastery that encourages further exploration and refinement of skills. In other words, marble painting for a day will produce some nice pictures. Marble painting for a week will result in increasingly complex paintings as the children learn to control the path of the marble and the placement and combination of paints. Give children the time they need and want, and you will see the results in increased focus, concentration, and discovery.

The Block Center

The Block Center, an essential part of the preschool classroom, is an exciting place to introduce children to discovery and investigation. A natural progression occurs as children develop their skills in the block area. Children begin by exploring the properties of blocks through pushing and carrying them. They move at their own rate along a continuum from flat structures and stacking on to enclosures, bridges, and decorated structures. An older preschool child who has had adequate experience with blocks is building complex, well-organized structures with plan and purpose. Other than basic safety and storage rules, few limits constrain the children as they work with blocks. They explore and challenge themselves, secure in the knowledge that they can always try it again. They work with problem-solving skills as they figure out how to support a ramp, reinforce a tower so they can build it higher, or decide which block will fit into a structure precisely.

As the children work in the block area they are learning about

- *Focusing Observations.* Children compare, observe, and handle the materials.

- *Observing to Classify.* Children sort by size, shape, color, or other attributes.

- *Organizing and Communicating Observations.* Children find ways to share their discoveries.

- *Balance.* Children carefully add blocks to buildings so they don't fall, and they employ visual balance as they make symmetrical structures.

- *Stability.* Children work, for example, to create the best form to enable them to build a taller building.

- *Spatial Relationships.* Children enclose, connect, bridge, and cover space or use blocks to fill containers.

- *Simple Machines.* Children manipulate levers, ramps, and pulleys.

The Dramatic Play Center

The Dramatic Play Center provides children with opportunities for role playing, trying out, pretending, and acting out familiar and imaginary experiences. They learn to interact with each other, to problem solve, and to communicate effectively. Young children often initially spend time manipulating objects and seeing how they work, just as they do in other areas of the classroom. They may play dress up, put a pot on the stove, or undress a doll. Gradually their play becomes more social as they assume various roles with each other. Dramatic play also provides the opportunity for children to explore how their bodies move and how they can vary those movements.

As the children work in this area, they are learning about

- *Focusing Observations.* Children use their senses to explore, experiment, and discover a diversity of textures, visual properties, and other characteristics of materials.

- *Observing to Classify.* Children compare shadows and movements that have similar characteristics.

- *Organizing and Communicating Observations.* Children find ways to share their discoveries and act out various roles.

- *Matching.* Children recognize shadows and movements that are alike and different.

- *Predicting.* Children describe what they think the shadows look like.

- *Constancy.* Children realize that mirror images remain the same as the objects that are reflected.

- *Change and Passage of Time.* Children realize how our activities change from day to night.

The Sand and Water Center

Sand and water, along with other materials such as rice, beans, and soil, are wonderful media for exploring a variety of science skills and experiences. The materials provide rich sensory experiences and are inherently attractive to children.

When children first work with fluid materials, such as sand or water, they need many opportunities to simply experience the substances and to learn to manage them. Even three-year-olds can learn to use a sponge or small broom if the equipment is available. Teaching the children management skills is necessary if wet and messy substances are to be welcome in the classroom.

Materials with fluidity provide many opportunities for children to become familiar with the use of tools such as double-pan balances, droppers, funnels, and sieves. In the early stages, children simply pour and scoop and fill and dump, all the while exploring the texture, smell, weight, and appearance of the material. They become absorbed in the tactile sensations. They learn the various uses of the equipment—cups, sieves, scoops—that you supply. They also learn that different materials behave in different ways with the same equipment. As they become familiar with the materials and equipment, play becomes more planned and organized. They learn that a sieve can be used to remove rocks from sand and that a funnel can assist in filling a small container.

An interested teacher can ask many kinds of questions to extend thinking: Are there some things that sink and float? How much water is the right amount to add to sand if you want to mold it?

As the children work with sand and water, they are learning about:

- *Focusing Observations.* Children compare, observe, and handle materials of varying textures, smells, and densities.

- *Observing to Classify.* Children sort by size, color, and shape.

- *Balance.* Children use a double-pan balance to make several comparisons.

- *Stability.* Children learn to center an object in a floating pie pan so it doesn't tip and sink.

- *Spatial Relationships.* Children work with volume, discovering that some containers hold more than others.

- *Physical Properties of Materials.* Children working with sand and water are challenged to think about volume, measurement, and comparison in concrete and meaningful ways.

The Discovery Center

The Discovery Center is the heart of Discovery Science. It contains all of the materials for using and continuing discovery begun in the other centers. The Discovery Center provides a place for children to begin to use the tools of science. Children can become proficient at using balances, magnifiers, and measurement devices while exploring here and in the other centers. Children need to use these tools with a wide variety of natural and human-made materials. They will see that the tools and materials in the Discovery Center consist of everyday items along with special "science" tools.

The children need many opportunities to make observations, classify those observations, and communicate data in an environment rich in materials, equipment, and experiences. The well-stocked Discovery Center can serve as both the hands-on area of new discoveries and the more traditional science center. Materials in the Discovery Center should be sturdy, simple, and easy to handle. If space does not allow for a permanent center, select materials that can be set up quickly and stored easily. The Discovery Center should contain the following basic equipment:

- safety goggles

- paint aprons or smocks

- magnifying devices such as hand lenses, bug boxes, and two-way magnifiers

- double-pan balance

- spoons, scoops, droppers, and forceps

- containers such as bowls, bottles, and cups

- sorting and storage containers such as egg cartons and clear plastic vials with lids

- cardboard or plastic foam food packaging trays for sorting and mess containment
- nonstandard units for measuring length and mass, such as animal counters, large metal washers, measuring cups, and interlocking cubes
- writing materials
- cleanup equipment, such as buckets, sponges, dust pans, and hand brooms

As the children work in the Discovery Center, they are learning about:

- *Focusing Observations.* Children use their senses to explore the natural and human-made objects in the center.
- *Observing to Classify.* Children learn to classify collections of objects according to a variety of characteristics.
- *Organizing and Communicating Observations.* Children share observations and discoveries with each other and with you.
- *Balance.* Children work with different types of balances.
- *Physical Properties of Materials.* Children explore and manipulate the tools and materials.
- *Quantification.* Children use standard and nonstandard measuring devices to quantify objects.

Small Group Activities

Activities labeled as Small Group activities are done with a small group of children at a time. While the rest of the children are working in other centers or on other activities, the teacher, aide, or resource person replicates the activity with each small group until every child has an opportunity to participate. Each child will thus have the rich experience of interacting with the materials and ideas being presented and with the teacher.

Going Outdoors: Nature's Center

Children find the natural world enchanting. They have an insatiable curiosity about their environment. The creative teacher can capitalize on this enthusiasm with developmentally appropriate experiences designed to challenge and extend their learning. The outdoor world provides a whole new avenue for exploring the themes of Discovery Science. Take advantage of the wealth of resources available in just about any outdoor environment.

The importance of environmental education in early childhood programs is a reflection of the concern about environmental issues and the future of our planet. At this age, environmental education provides children with the knowledge, skills, and attitudes required to take environmentally responsible actions. These actions will prevent further destruction and promote development of a sustainable society, thus ensuring the future of life on the earth. Nurturing attitudes and actions at an early age leads to environmentally responsible adults.

Introduce Going Outdoors time by taking the children to a somewhat private location on the school grounds. Talk with them about safety concerns and the importance of staying close enough to hear directions you may give. This is also an appropriate time to discuss environmental issues, such as littering and respect for living things. Often, for example, children will want to pick flowers rather than leave them so others can enjoy their beauty.

During this time the children may investigate the area at their own pace in their own way. They need this freedom to discover on their own so when they are later asked to focus on certain outdoor features or activities, they will be less likely to wander off to explore on their own.

Most of the Going Outdoors time will be spent in the area around your school. Visiting other places to do some of the activities is also fun. Field trips to woods, prairies, and shallow creeks can be big adventures for young children. Climbing a small hill becomes a major mountain-climbing expedition for a 36-inch-tall person. Once again, stress safety and environmental stewardship during your visits, and use field trips as opportunities to discuss environmental issues.

As the children work and explore outdoors, they are learning about:

- *Focusing Observations.* Children use their senses to explore, investigate, and discover the wealth of materials that nature provides.

- *Observing to Classify.* Children classify the wide variety of things they collect outdoors.

- *Organizing and Communicating Observations.* Children tally their collections, share their thoughts about what they see, and dictate captions for their work.

- *Balance and Stability.* Children work with the concepts of balance and stability as they walk on logs.

- *Spatial Relationships.* Children use their sense of spatial relationships as they choose how to place objects to make prints on paper.

- *Physical Properties of Materials.* Children discover the incredible variety of sights, textures, and smells in nature.

- *Change and Passage of Time.* Children observe changes in the natural environment throughout the year.

ASSESSMENT IN DISCOVERY SCIENCE

Assessment is a general term, with a variety of connotations for different groups of educators. The most widely accepted use of the word is in reference to tests used to collect information. Such information can be used by decision makers for the evaluation of individual children or an entire educational program.

Unfortunately the words *assessment* and *evaluation* conjure up visions of child and teacher confrontations and often are viewed as an afterthought to instruction and learning. For the assessment and the resulting evaluation of early childhood science to be of practical value, an authentic approach to assessment must be used.

The assessment and evaluation procedures used in Discovery Science are consistent with sound test and measurement approaches. They have been developed to be practical and informative for an early childhood teacher in the classroom setting. Assessment and evaluation in Discovery Science are tied closely to instruction and are embedded in the learning cycle, eliminating many of the ill effects of a "tacked on" caboose at the end of the train. Several train engines are spread throughout the long line of cars, engines that will give power and purpose to the learning activities.

Authentic Assessment

As educators we are interested in improving children's skills and expanding their knowledge of the world. To be sure our efforts in education are accomplishing the intended purpose, we need to monitor children's development continually. Ongoing educational assessment should be consistent with the instructional approach being used in the classroom and not an inappropriate, high-stakes assessment measure so foreign to the way children process information that it creates frustration and stress.

When assessment measures are tied closely to curriculum and the instructional approach used in the learning environment, we say that it is *authentic*. Discovery Science uses authentic assessment measures in such a way that both teachers and children perceive the assessment as an extension of the learning process.

Be aware of the diversity of the developmental levels of children in your classroom. Nothing in your evaluation should discourage children in the growth of their inquiry skills or, even worse, set their present attitude against scientific inquiry—an attitude they may well possess the rest of their lives. The development of a willingness to think, to explore, and to look for answers to questions is critically important for the proper development of good problem-solving skills.

The assessment system used in Discovery Science has three components: the Success in Science Inventory, Curriculum-Embedded Assessment, and the use of Discovery Charts. Following are descriptions of each form of assessment, the procedure used, and the type of information gained.

Success in Science Inventory

The Success in Science Inventory, or SSI, is a checklist used to record children's dispositions toward scientific inquiry. When certain behaviors or choices are made by a child, we begin to formulate an understanding of the level of interest and enthusiasm that child has for discovery. Although the SSI may be used at any time in the curriculum, we recommend it be used during each unit's Free Discovery period to assess the children's interaction with materials in the center and with each other. Evaluate each child in the four categories throughout the year. The suggested levels of performance are Not Apparent, Emerging, and Developed. A scale of 1 to 3 is suggested to simplify scoring.

The SSI will give you a picture of how the children are progressing overall. You will know that discovery is successful when these early problem-solving behaviors emerge in the children. You will also get a feel for when it is time to move on to the next phase of Discovery Science as you observe their behavior. The children will show that they are ready to do more.

The SSI assesses four science dispositions.

1. The child manipulates objects for useful observations.
   Does the child explore new materials placed in the Discovery Center in a thoughtful way?

2. The child seeks a clear understanding of the questions who, what, where, and when—the facts.
   When observing something unique on a field trip, does the child ask relevant questions?

3. The child seeks reasons: asks the question why and tries to answer it through further exploration.
   As a child builds a block structure that continues to fall down, does the child persist in trying alternatives?

4. The child communicates the results of observations and investigations.
   Does the child talk with you or others about Discovery Science activities?

Follow these guidelines for using the SSI:

1. Administer the SSI during each Free Discovery session. You may elect to observe and record dispositions for all children each time or to select certain children at different times.
2. Observe and record children's behavior in each of the four science themes.
3. Indicate the child's level within a particular disposition.

Curriculum-Embedded Assessment: Observing the Children

All too often assessment and evaluation are a completely separate phase of the learning experience. Unfortunately, when assessment is separated from instruction, the evaluation shifts from being formative and supportive to judgmental and, sometimes, even a ranking of the children. Eventually, separation of assessment from instruction sends a clear message to children: "Now I am supposed to be learning. Now I am supposed to be testing and *not* learning." By embedding the assessment in the activity, we don't abruptly stop a child's learning process.

Observing the Children is found at the end of each activity. This is an embedded evaluation that provides useful insight about how the children are developing skills and understanding concepts.

Discovery Charts

When created at the beginning of a unit, Discovery Charts can serve as a preassessment. They tell you what the children as a whole already know and can make you aware of misconceptions. When you take the time to refer back to an old chart, to add to it, or to create a new one, children will see clearly that they are learning. By making the Discovery Charts an ongoing part of Discovery Science, they will contain the main body of knowledge generated by the children.

Success in Science Inventory

	Science Dispositions				
Child's Name	**1**	**2**	**3**	**4**	**Comments**

1. Manipulates objects for useful observations.

2. Seeks a clear understanding of the questions who, what, where, when—the facts.

3. Seeks reason. Asks the question why and tries to answer it through further explorations.

4. Communicates the results of observations and investigations.

How Objects Are Alike and Different

The significance of this unit, How Objects Are Alike and Different, in the development of a child's scientific discovery skills cannot be overemphasized. The activities in this unit guide children in formulating a basic understanding of the meaning of the words *alike* and *different*.

Even more importantly, the activities encourage children to develop their focused observation skills to discover unique characteristics of various materials. Once children have experience with the concepts *alike* and *different*, they can use their new skills for the sophisticated challenge of sorting and grouping objects.

Several activities focus on the science process skill "to use observations to classify." These activities look at major differences and similarities among objects. As activities for each classroom center progress, the differences and similarities of the properties children are asked to compare become more subtle and therefore more difficult. Eventually children will be asked to use similarities and differences for basic classification activities such as sorting and grouping.

Science Concepts

The following science concepts will be addressed in this unit:

1. Many objects in our world have similar characteristics.

2. Many objects in our world have different characteristics.

3. We can use the similarities and differences of objects to separate them into groups.

Getting Ready

Place the following materials in the Discovery Center for the children to explore during Free Discovery:

- variety of objects to show *alike* and *different*

- large sheet of newsprint (for a Discovery Chart)

- markers

- magnets

- materials attracted to and not attracted to magnets

- texture collection, such as various fabrics, window screen, sandpaper, pieces of wood, and tiles

- objects to sort, such as buttons, marbles, coins, counters, rocks, and shells

- leaf collection

- pattern blocks

- insect collection

- nut and bolt collection

- feather collection

- pairs of objects, such as rocks, shells, and nuts

Organizing and Presenting the Unit

Phase 1: Free Discovery

Begin Free Discovery by discussing with a small group of children how various objects are alike and different. Bring a collection of objects to the group time. Ask the children to select things that are alike and to tell why. Ask them to do the same with objects that are different.

As the children share their thoughts, write them on a How Objects Are Alike and Different Discovery Chart.

Phase 2: Conducting the Activities

The second phase of Discovery Science takes place in your classroom learning centers (described in the section on the classroom centers). Use whatever approach to center management that you have found effective. The activities in this unit are general descriptions of developmentally appropriate activities for several traditional centers. Since the children will be varied in their level of cognitive development and physical maturity, offer a wide selection of activities. Choose the activities that are appropriate for your group.

Allow the children ample opportunities to investigate as many of the centers as possible, based on your time and space limitations. Some teacher assistance may be required to initiate the experience, but be careful not to over-direct the children.

Now is the time to initiate the class Discovery Books for this unit. You may want to use several books, each focused on a specific activity; a general book with drawings and captions showing what the children are learning about how objects are alike and different; or both.

As the children do the activities in the unit, encourage them to share their discoveries with you and add them to the How Objects Are Alike and Different Discovery Chart.

Phase 3: Making Connections to the Real World

The final phase of Discovery Science applies what the children have been experiencing in the classroom related to the concepts *alike* and *different* to the real world. Incorporate a field trip into this unit so the children may observe these concepts firsthand. Possible field trips might be a trip to the supermarket or department store, where a variety of similar and different objects can be compared.

Language and Reading Center

Before you begin this unit, visit the library to select appropriate books and other resource materials to place in the Language and Reading Center. Posters and tapes will also add interest to the area, as will the display of Discovery Books, Discovery Charts, and other examples of the children's work during the unit. A number of books appropriate for this age level are listed here.

Tail Toes Eyes Ears Nose by Marilee Robin Burton. New York: HarperCollins Children's Books, 1988.

Children guess the animal from its tail, toes, eyes, ears, and nose, and see the whole animal to check their answer on the next page. Final pages have groups of animal parts to help young readers classify.

This Is My House by Arthur Dorros. New York: Scholastic, 1992.

The lovely illustrations take us into the homes around the globe showing us how they are alike yet different.

But Not Like Mine by Margery Facklam. San Diego, Calif.: Gulliver Books/Harcourt, Brace, Jovanovich, 1988.

This book is a repetitive pattern through which readers make comparisons between the animal part and the human correlative hidden under a flap.

Whose Baby Am I? by Shirley Greenway. Nashville, Tenn.: Ideals Publishing.

The photograph on each page shows a mother animal with her baby. Some pairs look exactly alike, yet other youngsters look quite different from their parents.

Hats, Hats, Hats by Ann Morris. New York: Lothrop, Lee and Shepard Books, 1989.

The title says it all. Photographs show how hats are the same— for example soft—yet different all over the world.

People by Peter Spier. New York: Doubleday and Company, 1988.

Page after page is loaded with Spier's detailed illustrations depicting people from all over the world in hundreds of different activities.

ACTIVITY 1

Draw It—A Matter of Scale

Materials

paper (1 sheet per child)

crayons

two similar objects, one large and one small, such as 2 rocks, 2 balls, or 2 plants

large sheet of newsprint and markers (for a Discovery Chart)

This activity introduces two terms that define differences: *large* and *small*. The concepts are reinforced when children draw a large object and a small one. The drawings may not be realistic, but even very young children can indicate size differences in their work.

What to Do

1. Place the two objects in the Art Center.

2. Talk with the children about which object is large and which is small. You may also want to use the words *big* and *little*. Ask them to tell you about how the objects are alike and different.

3. Have the children fold their papers in half and draw the large object on one side of the paper and the small object on the other side. Encourage the children to use comparative language as they observe the two objects.

C ▪ O ▪ N ▪ N ▪ E ▪ C ▪ T ▪ I ▪ O ▪ N ▪ S

To Language

Expressive Language - Children will use comparative language as they observe the two objects.

Discovery Chart - You will make two lists of words to describes big and small things.

To Math

Measurement - Children will visually compare objects by size.

Science Concept

We can use the similarities and differences of objects to separate them into groups.

Science Process Skill

To focus observations by using the senses.

Science Vocabulary

alike, different, same

big, little

large, small

size

4. Have the children tell you which drawing is of the large object and which represents the small object. Label the drawings for the children, using their own words.

5. Make a Discovery Chart that has two lists of words— one that describes big things and one that describes small things. Some words the children might use are *teeny, tiny, itsy bitsy, gigantic, humongous,* and *really, really, really big.*

Observing the Children

Do the children's drawings, though they may be unrecognizable, reflect the difference in size?

ACTIVITY 2

When You Feel This Art

Materials

collection of materials with a variety of textures such as sand, gravel, sticks, beans, fabric, and textured paper

heavy paper or tag board (1 per child)

glue

large box with a hole cut in the side

When children create something, they can usually find their own work among others when it is time to take the project home. They identify it as different from other children's creations by sight. Use this tactile experience to make children aware of the sense of touch as another way of identifying differences.

What to Do

1. Show the children how to make their tactile art projects by putting glue on the paper and then adding various materials.

2. Be sure the children's names are on their work. Allow the texture collages to dry thoroughly.

3. Working with a small group, say to the children: Can you tell which collage is yours? Our eyes help us know which artwork is ours. Now we are going to see if our fingers can help us find our work.

C▪O▪N▪N▪E▪C▪T▪I▪O▪N▪S

To Language

Expressive Language - Children will describe what they feel as they touch their texture collages.

Science Concept

Many objects in our world have different characteristics.

Science Process Skill

To focus observations by using the senses.

Science Vocabulary

alike, different, same

collage

descriptive words such as rough, smooth, bumpy

feel

touch

4. Have the children feel their own texture collages until they are sure they can identify them. Help them talk about what they feel. Support their choice of words, and supply other words to expand their vocabularies.

5. Place two texture collages in the box. Have a child reach in and try to identify which is his or her collage. Lift the box to see if the choice is correct. As the children become more skilled, you may want to use more than two texture collages at a time.

Observing the Children

Can the children identify their own work? Are they using descriptive language?

ACTIVITY 3

Leaf-Shape Paintings

Materials

paper

tempera paints

paintbrushes

tape

leaves

paper towels (for clean up)

Every branch of a particular tree species has leaves that are very similar, yet each individual leaf has slight differences. There are much greater differences between leaves of different species. As the children make their paintings, help them focus on how the leaf shapes are alike and different.

Before the Activity

Gather a large collection of various types of leaves. Tell the children to bring in a few leaves from home for this activity. You might want to take a leaf-collecting walk with the children. Encourage variety in their collections.

What to Do

1. Display the collected leaves. Tell the children the names of the leaves you know. Support their use of color, size, texture, and shape words to describe the leaves.

C▪O▪N▪N▪E▪C▪T▪I▪O▪N▪S

To Language

Expressive Language - Children will use the names of the leaves and use color, size, texture, and shape words to describe the leaves.

To Math

Matching - Children match their leaf shapes with other children's paintings.

Science Concepts

Many objects in our world have similar characteristics.

Many objects in our world have different characteristics.

Science Process Skill

To focus observations by using the senses.

Science Vocabulary

alike, different, same

descriptive words for leaves, such as pointed, round, smooth, round, saw-toothed

leaf

match

shape

2. Show the children how to make a leaf-shape painting. Put a leaf on a piece of paper, and hold it in place with a small piece or two of tape. Paint all around the leaf, stroking outward from the center of leaf to the paper. Remove the leaf, and a print of the leaf shape will remain.

3. Let the children make their own leaf-shape paintings. Provide help if needed.

4. Talk with the children about leaf shapes and sizes. Ask questions to help them compare their leaf-shape paintings. Ask: Are they made from the same or different types of leaves?

5. Encourage the children to try to find a friend who has a leaf shape that matches theirs (optional).

Observing the Children

Can the children talk about how the leaves are alike and different?

ACTIVITY 4

The World in Different Colors

Materials

cardboard tubes (2 per child)

plastic wrap in different colors

rubber bands (3 or 4 per child)

large sheet of newsprint and markers
(for a Discovery Chart)

Make the world a different color! The children create their own color viewers with cardboard tubes, colored plastic wrap, and rubber bands. They will begin to discover that things can be alike and different at the same time.

What to Do

1. Begin this activity by giving each child a cardboard tube, rubber bands, and different colors of plastic wrap. Show them how to use the rubber band to hold the plastic wrap over the end of the tube. Some of the children may need help with this.

2. Ask: How do the things in the room change when you look through the tube?

3. Have children use a second tube to repeat the process with a different color of plastic. Now comes the fun part. Have the children take another rubber band or two and connect the tubes together like binoculars. Ask: Now what color are all the objects in the room? Do the colors change?

C ▪ O ▪ N ▪ N ▪ E ▪ C ▪ T ▪ I ▪ O ▪ N ▪ S

To Language

Expressive Language - Children will practice their use of color words.

Discovery Chart - You will list how the color tubes change certain colors.

Science Concept

We can use the similarities and differences of objects to separate them into groups.

Science Process Skill

To focus observations by using the senses.

Science Vocabulary

alike, different, same

change

color words

4. Try other combinations. Have the children look with one eye and then with the other eye. (Many children this age find it hard to close one eye at a time. Show them how to cover one eye with their hand.) Talk with them about the similar colors and difference in colors between tubes. Also talk about the differences in colors when both eyes remain open.

5. Have the children dictate lists of things in the room that are yellow, blue, or red. Put the lists on a Discovery Chart. Talk about how the color tubes change the color of the items on the lists.

Observing the Children

Do the children realize that the appearances of some objects change when viewed through the different color tubes?

ACTIVITY 5

Crayon Lines

Materials

many crayons of two different colors, such as red and yellow

masking tape

items for sorting, such as blocks

In this activity you will ask the children to find crayons that are alike—that are of the same color—then to sort them and line them up by color. Once the children have lined up the crayons, they will immediately be able to tell which color has the most crayons.

What to Do

1. Have the children sort the crayons by color into two separate piles. Say: Which color do you think will make the longest line? Let's find out.

C ▪ O ▪ N ▪ N ▪ E ▪ C ▪ T ▪ I ▪ O ▪ N ▪ S

To Language

Expressive Language - Children will use color names as they sort and line up the crayons. They will use comparative language as they talk about which line is the longest, which color has the most number of crayons, and so on.

To Math

Sorting - Children will group the crayons by color.

Measurement - Children will use the length of the crayon lines to compare the quantity of crayons in the two colors.

Graphing - The crayon lines will form a simple bar graph.

ART CENTER

Science Concept

We can use the similarities and differences of objects to separate them into groups.

Science Process Skill

To use observations to classify.

Science Vocabulary

color names

graph

group

line

longest

measure

most

sort

2. Place a long piece of masking tape on the floor. Show the children how to line up the crayons of one color end to end along the tape.

3. When all the crayons of that color are lined up, mark the spot where the crayon line ends by making a line with that color on the tape.

4. Have the children repeat the process with the second color along the same piece of tape.

5. When both colors have been measured, ask the children which color made the longest line.

6. Encourage the children to use the same process with other colors or with other objects, such as blocks.

7. Send home How Objects Are Alike and Different Family Connection Activity 1 (page 333).

Observing the Children

Can the children separate the two colors accurately? Can they tell you which color made the longest line? Can they apply the same process to other materials?

Sticky Painting

Some materials adhere better than others. Heavier objects may not stay in place as well as lighter objects. Some things may not have sufficient surface area to adhere. When the children experiment with a variety of materials, they will discover this and more for themselves.

Materials

dry sand

dry soil

assorted materials to sprinkle on paintings, such as rice, dried beans, and beads

small cups

paper (1 sheet per child)

paintbrushes

washable white glue

food coloring

Before the Activity

Prepare colored glue in a variety of colors using washable white glue and food coloring.

What to Do

1. Have the children paint pictures with the colored glue.

2. Let them choose which of the materials they would like to sprinkle on their pictures. After adding the material, they shake the excess off into a trash can.

C ▪ O ▪ N ▪ N ▪ E ▪ C ▪ T ▪ I ▪ O ▪ N ▪ S

To Language

Expressive Language - Children will talk about what happens and use texture words as they work with the materials.

To Math

Comparing - Children will compare how well the various materials stick to the glue as they create their paintings.

ART CENTER

Science Concept

Many objects in our world have many different characteristics.

Science Process Skill

To use observations to classify.

Science Vocabulary

alike, different, same

stick, sticky

texture words, such as bumpy, sticky, crumbly, rough, smooth

3. As the children try different materials, they will observe which materials adhere to the glue best. Ask them to share their observations and thoughts as to why some materials adhere better than others. Help the children focus on texture words and other descriptive language.

4. Help the children identify some of the characteristics of things that adhere well and of things that do not.

Observing the Children

Can the children identify some materials that adhere to the paper better than others? Talk with them about what happens when they hang up their pictures.

ACTIVITY 7

Insects and Worms— What's the Difference?

Animals provide a wonderful way to explore similarities and differences. Most insects have legs. Most worms do not. Both creatures are small and both can move. Help the children identify other similarities and differences.

Materials

live insects

live worms

variety of materials for constructions, such as clay, straws, pipe cleaners, toothpicks, and buttons

moistened paper towel

large sheet of newsprint and markers (for a Discovery Chart)

Before the Activity

Obtain live insects and worms. If you cannot find any yourself, check bait or pet stores.

What to Do

1. Prepare the Art Center with a rich variety of materials for constructing insects and worms.

2. Display several different live insects in the classroom. Talk with the children about the insects' various physical characteristics, such as legs, eyes, and bodies.

C▪O▪N▪N▪E▪C▪T▪I▪O▪N▪S

To Language

Discovery Chart - Children will compare the various characteristics of worms and insects.

ART CENTER

Science Concepts

Many objects in our world have different characteristics.

Many objects in our world have similar characteristics.

Science Process Skill

To use observations to classify.

Science Vocabulary

alike, different, same

alive

animal

body part names

insect

insect names

worm

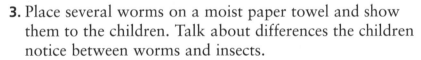

3. Place several worms on a moist paper towel and show them to the children. Talk about differences the children notice between worms and insects.

4. Encourage each child to construct both an insect and a worm in the Art Center. Talk with them about the physical differences between insects and worms.

5. Prepare an area with a sign for "Insects" to be displayed and another labeled area for "Worms."

6. Make a Discovery Chart. Have the children dictate characteristics of the worms and of the insects. Ask: Are there any that are the same?

Observing the Children

Does each child's worm and insect reflect the differing characteristics? For example, does the insect have legs and the worm have none?

ACTIVITY 8

Paint It If You Can

Materials

water-based paints

paintbrushes (2 per child)

painting sheets (see Before the Activity)

paper towels (for clean up)

Paint adheres to some surfaces better than it adheres to other surfaces. This activity gives children an opportunity to discover that fact for themselves. Let them explore freely with a great variety of materials.

Before the Activity

Create the painting sheets by cutting a variety of materials —such as waxed paper, aluminum foil, plastic wrap, cardboard, newspaper, slick magazine paper, construction paper, and finger-paint paper—into roughly 9-inch or 12-inch squares. The greater the variety of materials you offer, the more interesting this activity will be.

What to Do

1. Place all of the materials in the Art Center. Encourage the children to paint on the different painting sheets.

C·O·N·N·E·C·T·I·O·N·S

To Language

Expressive Language - Children will talk about what happens to the paint on various surfaces.

To Math

Grouping - Children will group the painting sheets by those paint will and won't adhere to.

ART CENTER

Science Concept

Many objects in our world have different characteristics.

Science Process Skill

To use observations to classify.

Science Vocabulary

material names

sort

description words such as runny, smear, and puddle

2. After the children have had some time to explore the materials, discuss their observations. Ask: What materials did you like to use for painting? Are there some that did not work? Build the children's vocabularies by using the names of the materials you used to make the painting sheets.

3. Encourage the children to talk about what happens to the paint on various surfaces. They might use words such as *puddle, runny, smear,* and *it messes up.*

4. Have the children sort their sheets by those paint adheres to and those it does not adhere to.

Observing the Children

Do the children choose some materials as better to paint on than others? Do they identify some materials that do not work?

ACTIVITY 9

My Color Book

Materials

resealable plastic bags (several per child)

stapler

magazines

scissors (1 per child)

masking tape

three-ring binder (optional)

Each child doing this activity will create a book with resealable bags. The books will all be different, because each child will have a unique approach to selecting pictures. The colors, however, will be the same within each book. The children will explore similarities and differences among the books.

C ▪ O ▪ N ▪ N ▪ E ▪ C ▪ T ▪ I ▪ O ▪ N ▪ S

To Language

Expressive Language - Children will name the objects pictured in their books.

ART CENTER

Science Concept

Many objects in our world have similar characteristics.

Science Process Skill

To use observations to classify.

Science Vocabulary

alike, different, same

color words

names of objects in books

What to Do

1. Let the children choose the color of the book they will make. Have them search through the magazines and tear or cut pictures containing primarily that color.

2. Help them place the colored pictures into the bags. Seal and staple several bags together to form books. Label each book with the color.

3. Have the children name some of the objects pictured in their books. Do books for different colors have some of the same objects? Do books for the same colors have different objects?

4. The children can take the books home and add additional pages with help from their families.

5. A three-ring binder can be used to make a class color book.

Observing the Children

Look for accuracy in the colors of objects the children have placed in their books.

ACTIVITY 1

Block Sandwiches

Materials

unit blocks, pattern blocks, or other sets of blocks with a variety of shapes

Making sandwiches gives the children a simple metaphor to work with as they explore the relationships of block shapes. This simple building model can be used later as the children begin making more complex structures.

What to Do

1. Encourage the children to talk about their favorite sandwiches and what goes into them. Let them pretend to make them with the blocks. Talk about all the different favorite sandwiches. It might be fun to make some of the sandwiches for snack time using the children's recipes.

2. Tell the children they will play a game making layered sandwiches. Place a block on the floor. Say: This is the bread. Ask a child to cover it *exactly* with other different-shaped blocks. For example, with unit blocks, four triangles cover the standard rectangle. The child can name this "layer." For example, the child could call it "peanut butter."

C ▪ O ▪ N ▪ N ▪ E ▪ C ▪ T ▪ I ▪ O ▪ N ▪ S

To Language

Expressive Language - Children will talk about their favorite sandwiches and what goes into them.

To Math

Matching - Children will make the same shape again and again from different shapes. They will realize that some sets of blocks are not compatible with others for this activity.

Science Concepts

Many objects in our world have similar characteristics.

Many objects in our world have different characteristics.

Science Process Skill

To focus observations by using the senses.

Science Vocabulary

alike, different, same

fit

layer

match

mix

sandwich

shape words

3. Ask: Can you make another layer for this sandwich? How about some "jelly"?

4. Continue to encourage the child to find out whether there are more possibilities. Once children understand the concept, they can play the sandwich game with each other.

5. Have them play the sandwich game with several different sets of blocks. Ask: Are there sets of blocks that will work when mixed together? Are there some sets that will not work together?

Observing the Children

Are the children able to use a variety of combinations to cover the same area? Do they understand that some blocks are proportionately related (fit together) and others are not? Are they able to point out sandwiches that look alike or look different?

ACTIVITY 2

Fill in the Blanks

Materials

unit blocks, pattern blocks, or other sets of blocks with a variety of shapes

cardboard shapes (see Before the Activity)

This activity is a simplified version of tangram activities. It uses cardboard shapes and blocks to create a versatile puzzle activity for children.

Before the Activity

You will need a few large cardboard boxes from which to cut cardboard pieces. Arrange the blocks in a variety of simple shapes, then trace the shapes on the cardboard and cut them out. Make some patterns using the larger blocks and some using the smaller blocks. Make two cutouts of some of the cardboard shapes.

What to Do

1. Have the children use the blocks to fill in the cardboard shapes. Talk with the children about the fact that different children may fill the same shapes in the same or different ways. Ask children who have filled in identical shapes whether they used the same blocks in the same way.

C▪O▪N▪N▪E▪C▪T▪I▪O▪N▪S

To Language

Expressive Language - Children will use the names of the shapes.

To Math

Matching - Children will match the blocks to the cardboard shapes.

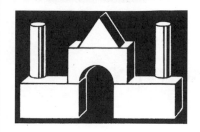

Science Concepts

Many objects in our world have similar characteristics.

Many objects in our world have different characteristics.

Science Process Skill

To focus observations by using the senses.

Science Vocabulary

layers

match

most

set

shape words

smallest, largest

2. Encourage the children to find as many ways as they can to fill the various shapes. Ask them to top the first layer of blocks with another layer using a new combination of blocks. Encourage the children to talk about the names of the shapes. For example, ask: Do you want me to hand you the square or the triangle?

3. When the children cover the same shape a second time, ask: Can you cover the shape with more blocks? How many different layers can you make? What happens if you use a different set of blocks?

Observing the Children

Do the children grasp the concept of covering an area as indicated by their ability to fill a cardboard shape exactly? Do you see increasing skill in their ability to accurately select a block that will fill a given space? Can they come up with new way of filling the same space?

ACTIVITY 3

Materials

unit blocks

other sets of blocks (optional)

large sheet of newsprint and markers
(for a Discovery Chart)

How Many Rectangles Can You Make?

In some ways, squares and rectangles are always the same. They always have four sides and four right-angle corners. However, they can be created in an infinite number of sizes. In this activity, children will begin to see that squares and rectangles can be used to create more squares and rectangles—and may find some blocks that cannot be used to make rectangles.

What to Do

1. Demonstrate to the children how they can arrange four blocks to make an outline of a rectangle.

2. Give the children several blocks and see if they can create more rectangle outlines. Encourage them to add on to the rectangles already made.

3. Talk with them about how more rectangles can be made by adding more blocks. Can they count the rectangles they have made?

C ▪ O ▪ N ▪ N ▪ E ▪ C ▪ T ▪ I ▪ O ▪ N ▪ S

To Language

Discovery Chart - You will list the square and the rectangular items the children see in the classroom.

To Math

Patterning - Children will develop a mental image of the pattern of a rectangle as they create it again and again in a variety of sizes.

Counting - Children will count rectangles they have made and the sides and corners of the rectangles.

Science Concept

Many objects in our world have similar characteristics.

Science Process Skill

To focus observations by using the senses.

Science Vocabulary

corner

larger, smaller

more

rectangle

shape

side

square

4. Count the sides and corners of the rectangles with the children. For example, say: Let's count the sides. Let's count the corners. You are right. It is a rectangle!

5. (optional) Ask: Can you find some blocks that cannot be used to make rectangles?

6. Work with the children to create a Discovery Chart listing all the things they can think of or see in the classroom that are shaped like squares or rectangles. The list might include window, book, door, cracker box, piece of bread, and stick of gum.

Observing the Children

Can the children find objects in the classroom shaped like a rectangle? Some of the children may realize that a rectangle has four sides and four corners.

ACTIVITY 4

Twin Towers

Materials

blocks

Building block structures that are either alike or different from a model employs the concepts *alike* and *different*. It also involves fine-motor skills and visual perception. The children will develop these skills as they are challenged by you or their friends to build something alike or different.

C•O•N•N•E•C•T•I•O•N•S

To Language

Expressive Language - Children will use color, size, and shape words as they talk about how their structures are alike or different.

To Math

Comparing - Children will use color, size, and shape to identify similarities and differences.

Science Concepts

Many objects in our world have similar characteristics.

Many objects in our world have different characteristics.

Science Process Skill

To focus observations by using the senses.

Science Vocabulary

alike, different, same

build

color, size, and shape words

construct

model

What to Do

1. Build a simple structure using three or four blocks. Ask: Can you make a tower that looks just like mine?

2. When the tower is complete, talk with the children about how this tower and yours are alike.

3. Ask the children to build towers that are different from yours.

4. Talk about the differences in the various towers. Ask: Are there any ways they are alike? Encourage the children to use color, size, and shape words as they talk about how their structures are alike or different. This will be a real challenge for many of the children.

5. Encourage the children to continue this activity with each other.

Observing the Children

Each child should be able to construct a simple tower that is alike or different. They may be able to tell you how they are alike or different.

ACTIVITY 1

Your Move

Materials

music (optional)

In this activity the children will use movement to explore the concepts *alike* and *different*. Tailor the activity to the ability levels of your children as you ask them to move as you do or in a different way.

What to Do

1. Have the children stand in front of you. Move and ask them to move exactly as you are moving. Explain that you are all moving *alike*. Walk in place.

2. Change your movement to jumping, and say: Move just like me.

3. Explain that you can also say the word *different*. Say: When I use the word *different*, you cannot make the same movement I am making but must move differently.

4. Start jumping and say the word *different*. The children should be doing anything but jumping. Even standing still is different. The children may need suggestions at first.

5. Practice the game, moving through a sequence of activities mixing *alike* and *different* as you go. Have some of the children give the calls and lead the game. Choose a wide range of movements so children with varying levels of motor skills will be successful.

C▪O▪N▪N▪E▪C▪T▪I▪O▪N▪S

To Language

Expressive Language - Children will describe the different ways they are moving.

Science Concepts

Many objects in our world have similar characteristics.

Many objects in our world have different characteristics.

Science Process Skill

To focus observations by using the senses.

Science Vocabulary

alike, different, same

move

6. Ask the children to name the different ways they are moving such as hopping, clapping, and spinning. They could also describe variations in the same movement, such as jumping forward or backward.

7. You may want to repeat this activity another time with music.

Observing the Children

Do the children understand when they are to move *like* the leader and when they are to move *different* from the leader? (Note: Differences in motor skills may keep some children from moving exactly as the leader moves.)

ACTIVITY 2

Matching Shadows

Shadows change three-dimensional objects into two-dimensional shapes, and these shadows can be described as alike or different. The shadow setup gives children the opportunity to identify things as alike or different.

Materials

white sheet

length of rope

lamp

matched objects to place behind the sheet, such as chairs, blocks, lights, and boxes

Before the Activity

Use the sheet and rope to create a curtain so that objects, two children, and the lamp can be placed behind it.

What to Do

1. Show the children how shadows form on the screen when a light is placed behind it and an object is put between the light and the sheet. Go behind the screen and cast a shadow. Pick up two fairly large objects and hold them so they form shadows. Ask: Are the objects alike or different?

2. Have a child go behind the screen with you. Ask: Are our two shadows alike or different?

C ▪ O ▪ N ▪ N ▪ E ▪ C ▪ T ▪ I ▪ O ▪ N ▪ S

To Language

Expressive Language - Children will describe what they think some of the shadows look like.

To Math

Comparing - Children will compare the ways that they feel the shadows are alike and different.

Matching - Children will decide whether or not two shadows match.

Science Concepts

Many objects in our world have similar characteristics.

Many objects in our world have different characteristics.

Science Process Skill

To use observations to classify.

Science Vocabulary

alike, different, same

light

match

shadow

3. Have two children go behind the sheet and stand still. Go behind and tell them how to stand to get similar or different poses. When a pose is reached, ask the other children to tell whether the poses are alike or different.

4. Have pairs of children take turns and choose their own alike and different poses. At times during the activity, ask the children to complete the sentence, "That shadow looks like. . . ."

Observing the Children

Can the children tell you whether two shadows are alike or different?

ACTIVITY 1

Digging in the Sand

Materials

small objects, such as washers, marbles, plastic animals, toy cars, coins, pieces of paper, blocks, rocks, and sticks

box of sand or a water table filled with sand

In this activity, the children will use the sense of touch to explore in the sand table. As they burrow below the surface of the sand, object pairs will be discovered. Will they feel alike or different? Are they very different or almost alike? Pull them out and look: are you correct?

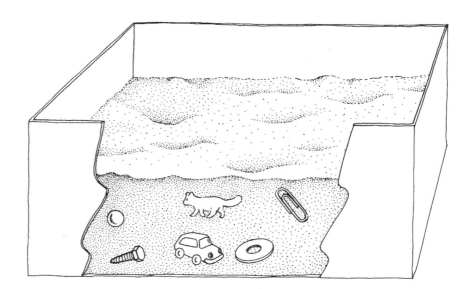

C▪O▪N▪N▪E▪C▪T▪I▪O▪N▪S

To Language

Expressive Language - Children will use comparative language as they talk about the objects that they feel are alike and different

To Math

Sorting - The children will sort objects into pairs that are alike and pairs that are different.

Science Concept

We can use the similarities and differences of objects to separate them into groups.

Science Process Skill

To focus observations by using the senses.

Science Vocabulary

alike, different, same

buried

sort

Before the Activity

Collect a number of objects that are alike and different, and bury the objects in the sand.

What to Do

1. Say: "Put your hands in the sand. Use your fingers to feel for two objects, one for each hand."
2. Ask: "Have you found something? Do the things you have found feel alike or different?"
3. The children answer and then pull up the objects, one in each hand, to immediately check their response.
4. Have children sort the objects they have pulled from the sand into pairs that are alike and pairs that are different.

Observing the Children

Are the children accurate in their response of whether the things are alike or different?

ACTIVITY 2

Dunk a Pair

Materials

clear plastic cups

water

pairs of objects such as sponges, rocks, shells, paper of various kinds, sugar cubes, cotton balls, coins, magnets, chalk, dirt, sand, and cloth

Water is an excellent medium for creating change. This activity asks the children to place one of a set of alike objects in water to discover how it is changed. The change made by contact with water may be quite obvious, as with crepe paper, or minimal, as with a penny.

What to Do

1. Show the children two objects that are alike. Make the first object something that will change when placed in water, like paper. Discuss how the objects are alike.

2. Show the children how to place one of the pair in a cup of water to test what water will do to the object. The dry object is for the children to make easy and direct observations.

C ▪ O ▪ N ▪ N ▪ E ▪ C ▪ T ▪ I ▪ O ▪ N ▪ S

To Language

Expressive Language - The children will describe the changes occurring to each of the objects.

To Math

Matching - Children will recognize matched pairs of objects.

Grouping - Children will see form two groups of objects based on their tests.

Counting - Children will count the objects in each set.

Science Concept

We can use the similarities and differences of objects to separate them into groups.

Science Process Skill

To use observations to classify.

Science Vocabulary

alike, different, same

compare

group

wet

3. Hold up the wet object. Discuss the change. Ask: "Was the change a big one or not much of a change?" Lay the pair on the table.

4. Now select a pair that will show little change, such as pennies. Try the object in water, and observe the change with the children. Little change should have taken place.

5. Compare the two changes, making two piles on the table: one for things that are changed easily by water and another for those that are not easily changed by water.

6. Have the children experiment with the pairs of alike objects by placing one of them in water.

7. After the exploration, have children share their observations with the group and place their pair of objects in the "easy to change by water" group or the "not easy to change by water" group.

8. Ask: "Are more object pairs in one group or the other?" With the children, count how many pairs are in each group.

Observing the Children

Can the children describe the changes taking place when the objects are placed in water? Are they able to place the pairs in the correct group?

ACTIVITY 1

Magnets Attract

Materials

magnets (1 per child)

assorted objects, some attracted by magnets and some that are not, such as paper clips, small plastic toys, nails, washers, pennies, and aluminum foil

paper bag (1 per group)

large sheet of newsprint and markers (for a Discovery Chart)

tape (optional)

Magnets can be used to separate objects into two groups—those attracted to magnets and those that are not. In this activity, children are encouraged to identify ways objects in the two groups are alike and different and to find things to add to the groups.

Before the Activity

Place a wide variety of objects in the paper bags. Objects should not have different parts that are attracted and not attracted to magnets. (For example, a ball-point pen may have both plastic and a metal clip.)

What to Do

1. Introduce the word *attract*. Most of the children will continue to say such things as, "The magnet *picked up* the nail," but they will have been introduced to a word

C▪O▪N▪N▪E▪C▪T▪I▪O▪N▪S

To Language

Expressive Language - Children will begin to use words that explain the phenomenon of magnetic pull.

Discovery Chart - You will list the items that a magnet does and does not pick up.

To Math

Classify - Children will classify the objects into groups of items attracted or not attracted to a magnet.

they will continue to hear when they work with magnets. It will also give them a word to use when they feel the pull of a magnet on something that the magnet cannot pick up, such as a file cabinet.

2. Show the children a magnet and two objects, one attracted to the magnet and the other not (such as a washer and a lima bean). Point to a bag and say: Some of the objects in this bag are like this washer. They are attracted to a magnet. Pick up the washer with the magnet, then say: Some objects will be different. The magnet will not pick them up. Demonstrate with the lima bean.

3. Place the bags of objects on tables. Have the children work in groups to sort the objects into the two groups.

4. As the children sort, they will discover that magnets will consistently attract (iron containing) metal objects. The magnets always react the same way to those objects. They also react consistently to nonmagnetic objects.

5. Talk about the two groups. Each group contains objects that are like each other, and the two groups are different from each other. Ask the children to find other things to add to each group.

6. Make a Discovery Chart. As the children dictate, list items a magnet picks up on one side of the chart and those it does not on the other side. You may want to tape objects on the chart.

7. Send home How Objects Are Alike and Different Family Connection Activity 2 (page 333).

Observing the Children

Can the children test an item with a magnet and place it in the correct group? Some children may be able to tell you how a washer and a nail are alike.

Science Concept

We can use the similarities and differences of objects to separate them into groups.

Science Process Skill

To use observations to classify.

Science Vocabulary

alike, different, same

attract

group

magnet

sort

ACTIVITY 2

How Do They Go Together?

Materials

plastic animals, plastic fruit, rocks, beans, nuts, shells, or other sets of objects with similar and different members in the group

Young children often begin to classify objects by themselves. They may group animals in the Block Center or put together manipulatives by color. This activity capitalizes on that inclination by encouraging them to sort collections of objects in a variety of ways.

What to Do

1. Lay all the objects you have collected in front of a small group of children. Begin to group the objects to capture the children's attention.

2. When the children are watching what you are doing, start moving the objects into sets of similar shapes, colors, or sizes.

C·O·N·N·E·C·T·I·O·N·S

To Language

Expressive Language - Children will use the words *alike* and *different* as they talk about which things belong in a group and which do not. They will use descriptive words to explain their selections.

To Math

Classifying - You will work with the children to classify objects by a number of different attributes.

Counting - Some of the children may want to count the number of objects in each group.

Science Concept

We can use the similarities and differences of objects to separate them into groups.

Science Process Skill

To use observations to classify.

Science Vocabulary

alike, different, same

descriptive words of the objects

group

3. Ask the children to help you group the objects. Use the words *alike* and *different* and descriptions of the objects as you talk with them about their selections.

4. Sort the same group of objects another way. Follow the children's suggestions if they have any.

5. Repeat the activity with a large variety of objects. Encourage the use of descriptive words as you and the children group the objects by shape, size, or some other attribute.

6. Place the collections in the Discovery Center for the children to use independently.

Observing the Children

The children should be able to help you move objects into groups and use the words *alike* and *different* to explain their work.

ACTIVITY 3

Critter Matching

Materials

2 each of several of the following species (or whatever you can collect): pill bugs, slugs, snails, beetles, earthworms, houseflies, grasshoppers, fish, ants

paper and crayons (for a Discovery Book)

For this activity, you will need pairs of animals for the children to observe. You could use pictures, but using live animals is not that much trouble and is much more interesting. You will be giving the children an experience with caring for living things as they explore similarities and differences.

What to Do

1. Share the collection of various species with the children. Use this experience to develop the children's descriptive vocabularies. Give them plenty of time to touch, look at, and talk about the animals.

2. Ask the children if they can name any of the animals.

3. As the children examine the species, identify and discuss where the animal lives and what it eats to stay alive.

C▪O▪N▪N▪E▪C▪T▪I▪O▪N▪S

To Language

Expressive Language - Children will use descriptive vocabulary as they touch, look at, and talk about animals.

Discovery Book - Children will draw pictures of animals.

To Math

Matching - Children will match the species of animals and talk about the attributes that make them the same.

Science Concept

We can use the similarities and differences of objects to separate them into groups.

Science Process Skill

To use observations to classify.

Science Vocabulary

alike, different, same

animal

animal names

body part names

home

match

4. As the children interact with the animals, they will spot that there are two of each species. If they do not, pick up a species and ask the children to find another one like it.

5. After they have found a match, ask: How do you know they are alike? The children will probably respond with: "These two look the same," or "These two both have shells." Encourage them to come up with additional descriptive words. You may need to provide some ideas.

6. Ask: Can you think of some other animals you have seen? What about dogs and cats? In what ways do they look alike? In what ways do they look different?

7. Have the children help you return the animals to their homes.

8. Have the children each draw a picture of one of the animals and dictate a caption for it. Assemble the pages into a Discovery Book.

Observing the Children

This activity encourages the children to observe animals to determine characteristics that make them alike or different. They should be able to point out some of the characteristics and indicate whether the characteristics are alike or different.

ACTIVITY 4

Lid Turn and Match

Materials

variety of jars of different sizes with lids to match; several jars should have interchangeable lids

This sorting and classifying activity also develops fine-motor skills. You will be asking the children to sort jars into groups with like lids and to talk about what makes the groups alike or different.

C · O · N · N · E · C · T · I · O · N · S

To Language

Expressive Language - Children will be using comparative language as they talk about the different sizes of jars and lids. They will learn which lids and jars match or "go together."

To Math

Matching - Children will learn that the same lid can match different sizes of jars. This discovery may be an incongruity that they will have to prove to themselves over and over.

Grouping - Children will group the jars by matching lids.

Science Concept

We can use the similarities and differences of objects to separate them into groups.

Science Process Skill

To use observations to classify.

Science Vocabulary

alike, different, same

fit

group

match

What to Do

1. Place the jars, with lids removed, on a table or on the floor. Let the children predict which lid will fit which jar before they begin.

2. Have the children match the lids to the appropriate jars. After doing this self-correcting activity a number of times, the children will be able to tell you which lid fits which jar.

3. Once the children have become comfortable placing the lids on the jars, have them group the jars. All the jars in each group should be able to interchange lids.

4. Have the children test the lids to see if they are interchangeable with all the jars in a group.

Observing the Children

The children should be able to tell you why a particular jar is placed in a group of jars. You might provide a new jar and ask to which group it belongs.

ACTIVITY 5

Nuts and Bolts

Materials

nuts and bolts, with a variety of bolts that can be screwed into the same nut

paper bags

Using nuts and bolts gives children another experience with sorting objects that fit together. You will probably be able to build quite a collection simply by asking for families to send some nuts and bolts to school. The more diverse the collection, the more interesting this activity will be.

Before the Activity

Ask families to donate various sizes of bolts and nuts or collect them yourself. In each bag, place two nuts of two sizes. Also put in four to ten bolts of two sizes (but in a variety of shapes) that will fit one or the other of the two nuts. The number of bolts depends on your children's abilities. Also prepare more challenging bags with three or more different sizes of nuts and bolts in each bag.

C▪O▪N▪N▪E▪C▪T▪I▪O▪N▪S

To Language

Expressive Language - Children will use comparative terms as they match nuts to bolts.

To Math

Matching - Children will be matching the size of a bolt to the size of the opening in a nut. They may also find nuts and bolts that are the same shape and/or size.

Seriation - Some children will order nuts and bolts by size.

Science Concept

We can use the similarities and differences of objects to separate them into groups.

Science Process Skill

To use observations to classify.

Science Vocabulary

alike, different, same

fit

match

nut, bolt, screw

size

size-relationship terms

turn

What to Do

1. Have children pour their bags of nuts and bolts on the floor or table.

2. Tell the children to group the bolts by which nuts they will fit.

3. Have the children take one of the groups of bolts and screw them one at a time into the proper nut. Use comparative terms such as *smaller, too big, little,* and *the same size* as you work with the children.

4. Repeat with more difficult sets of nuts and bolts.

5. If the children are able, ask them to order the nuts and bolt by size from smallest to largest.

Observing the Children

Watch as the children sort the bolts. They should be able to determine that the size of a bolt and the size of the opening of a nut are the criteria for predicting which will fit together.

ACTIVITY 6

Feathers, Feathers

Materials

paper bags

assorted feathers (craft shops are a good source)

other sets of objects, such as shells and leaves

In this activity, the children will classify feathers. They may choose criteria you would not have thought of, such as pretty feathers not plain feathers. That they have criteria is more important than what their criteria are.

Before the Activity

Place a collection of feathers in each bag. A rich assortment of feathers will give you the opportunity to elicit language describing color, texture, and other characteristics.

What to Do

1. Provide the children with a bag of feathers of different colors, sizes, and shapes. Have the children sort them in some way. Encourage them to talk as they work, telling you why they are placing the feathers into groups as they are.

2. Ask the children to tell you why they chose to make the piles they did. Ask the children to finish this sentence: "All the feathers in this pile are alike because. . . ."

C ▪ O ▪ N ▪ N ▪ E ▪ C ▪ T ▪ I ▪ O ▪ N ▪ S

To Language

Expressive Language - Children will describe various characteristics of feathers as they sort them.

To Math

Grouping - Children will group feathers and other objects by common attributes.

Science Concept

We can use the similarities and differences of objects to separate them into groups.

Science Process Skill

To use observations to classify.

Science Vocabulary

alike

descriptions of feathers such as gray, soft, long

feather

group

match

sort

3. Go to a different pile and ask the same question.

4. Now ask the children to classify the feathers in a different way. Can they think of another way to make piles of feathers? If they have chosen color, show them how to use size.

5. Ask questions of each pile as you did before.

6. Give children another set of objects to sort, such as leaves. If using leaves, the children could glue one on top of the other when they find a match.

Observing the Children

Finishing the sentence allows the children to answer why the piles were formed. They should be able to apply the concept of *alike*.

ACTIVITY 1

The Touch Test

Materials

variety of pairs of materials children can hold in their palms, such as 2 rubber bands, 2 marbles, 2 shells, 2 blocks, 2 toy cars, 2 fabric squares, 2 vegetables, or 2 rocks

crepe paper for disposable blindfolds (optional)

Using the sense of touch is an effective way to reinforce the concepts alike and different. This is a simple game the children can play time and again with changing collections of objects.

C▪O▪N▪N▪E▪C▪T▪I▪O▪N▪S

To Language

Expressive Language - Children will use the words *alike* and *different* repeatedly in this game. They will also be encouraged to describe how objects feel.

To Math

Matching - Children will be ask to decide whether or not the objects match.

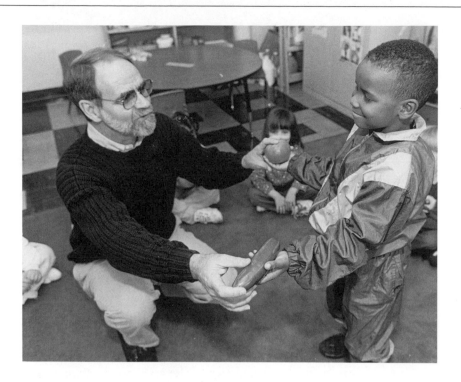

Science Concepts

Many objects in our world have similar characteristics.

Many objects in our world have different characteristics.

Science Process Skill

To focus observations by using the senses.

Science Vocabulary

alike, different

feel

match

pair

texture words

touch

What to Do

1. Gather the children into a circle. Ask one child to close his or her eyes or use a blindfold.

2. Place an object in each of the child's outstretched hands. Have the child tell you whether the objects are alike or different. Encourage the child to describe what he or she feels. (This will be difficult for most children. You may want to give choices such as, "Does it feel bumpy or smooth?")

3. Continue with the other children. Encourage the children to play the game with each other independently.

4. This activity can be made more complex by using different-colored objects of the same shape. They are alike with the eyes closed and *both* alike and different with the eyes open.

Observing the Children

Can the children correctly identify objects as alike or different?

ACTIVITY 2

Body Watch

Materials

music (optional)

This activity asks the children to look at themselves and others as they focus on what is alike and what is different about their characteristics. The activity provides you with the opportunity to talk with the children about how there are things that are alike and different about all of us and about how this is a positive part of life. Through movement, the children will work with what is the same and different about their own bodies.

What to Do

1. Talk with the children about their bodies. Ask: What parts of our bodies are the same? Responses will probably be eyes, teeth, fingers, fingernails, hair, legs, arms, ears, feet. (As in all discussions about bodies, be sensitive with the children about physical differences.)

2. You can focus further discussion on the fact that although we have the same kind of body parts, we also have different skin, hair, and eye color; height; and shape of arms, fingers, legs, and total body.

C▪O▪N▪N▪E▪C▪T▪I▪O▪N▪S

To Language

Expressive Language - Children will use body-part names and describe the comparisons they make.

To Math

Matching - Children will identify which of their body parts match and which of their body parts come in pairs.

Science Concepts

Many objects in our world have similar characteristics.

Many objects in our world have different characteristics.

Science Process Skill

To focus observations by using the senses.

Science Vocabulary

alike, different, same

body part names

match

pair

similar

3. Encourage the children to observe themselves and each other, looking for similarities and differences. This exercise reinforces the children's identification of body parts. You might also ask them to talk about what the various parts of our bodies do.

4. Now play a movement game. Say: "Blink your eyes. They are both the same. Wiggle your hands. They are both the same. Now move a hand and a foot. They are different."

5. Continue the game using many other pairs of body parts. This activity is fun to do with music.

Observing the Children

The children should indicate some body parts that are the same. Also ask them to indicate some differences among the children in the classroom.

ACTIVITY 3

What's Alike About Me?

Materials

Children are often aware of ways in which they are alike or different from other children. "Look, we both have stars on our shirts" or "We have the same shoes, but mine are black" are the kinds of comments they share with their friends or teachers. In this activity, these observations are used to form groups. The children may be surprised to find that they can belong to more than one group.

What to Do

1. Begin the activity by having the children explore what is the same and different about the way they look. Encourage the children to talk about how they are alike and different. Capitalize on commonalities that you see or hear them commenting on. Take this opportunity to discuss how we are all alike in many ways and yet each person is special and unique in their differences.

C▪O▪N▪N▪E▪C▪T▪I▪O▪N▪S

To Language

Expressive Language - Children will describe how they are alike and different.

To Math

Grouping - You will be helping the children group themselves by common characteristics.

Graphing - Children will make a living model of a bar graph to help them compare the size of the groups.

Science Concept

We can use the similarities and differences of objects to separate them into groups.

Science Process Skill

To use observations to classify.

Science Vocabulary

alike, different, same

graph

group

shortest, longest

2. Place some of the children in a group according to a shared characteristic. At this age it is usually best to group by just one attribute, such as children wearing shoes with laces and children wearing shoes without laces.

3. Once the groups are formed, line the children up to make a living model of a bar graph. This will help them to compare the relative size of the two groups. One of the easiest ways to form a human bar graph is to have two groups of children face each other. Starting at the same point, the children form two lines and sit cross-legged. This naturally spaces the children fairly evenly, and they can see which line is the longest.

4. Have the children try to discover what is the same about *everyone* in the group.

Observing the Children

Can the children identify a common characteristic within a group?

ACTIVITY 4

Attribute Game

Materials

large sheets of colored poster board

variety of other circular, square, and triangular objects

This is a basic classification activity. The children enjoy it all the more because they are working with shapes almost as big as they are.

Before the Activity

Cut out a set of triangles, circles, and squares that have 18-inch to 20-inch sides or diameters from different colors of poster board. Cut out another set of shapes that have 10-inch to 12-inch sides or diameters.

What to Do

1. Scatter the shapes within view of where you are working with a small group.

C▪O▪N▪N▪E▪C▪T▪I▪O▪N▪S

To Language

Expressive Language - Children will use shape and color names throughout this activity. Some children will know these words. Others will begin to learn them as they hear you and the other children using them.

To Math

Grouping - Children will group shapes by a number of attributes—size, shape, and color. They will begin to realize that the same objects can be grouped in different ways.

Matching - Children will match the color, shape, and size of objects.

Science Concept

We can use the similarities and differences of objects to separate them into groups.

Science Process Skill

To use observations to classify.

Science Vocabulary

color words

group

match

same, different

shape

sort

triangle, circle, square

2. Choose a shape and place it in a central position on the floor. Say to a child: Can you look around and find a shape that is like this one in some way? If this is the first time the children are working with this kind of grouping, they may need a more specific question such as, "Can you find a shape that is the same color as this one?" Have the child pick one shape and put it with the first shape.

3. Ask the child to state why a particular shape was added to the group. Ask: Why it is like the others? Continue the process with the other children.

4. When a grouping is complete—for example, we can't find any more that are like all of the others—scatter the shapes again. Now have the children sort them by a different attribute. Encourage the children to use the words *alike* and *different* as they group the shapes.

Observing the Children

Can the children express what is the same about a group of shapes? At a more complex level, some children may be able to state why a given shape does not belong in a group.

ACTIVITY 1

Walk-Around-the-Block Litter Safari

Materials

examples of litter

large litter bags

Some children may be aware of recycling and littering, but it is unlikely they understand the impact litter has on wildlife. Plastic that is discarded on the land may kill or maim animals in rivers and oceans as it is swept downstream by seasonal rains and floods. It is also a danger to birds. Walk any city street, and you will see our litter problem. You can help by teaching the children about the issue. Take the children to a place with little litter and one with much litter, and have them compare the two areas.

What to Do

1. Talk to the children about the word *litter*. In other words, find out what they know. Ask: Do you know what litter is? Show them some examples of litter. Talk about how some litter can be dangerous to them and to some animals.

2. Take a walk around your building, and let the children point out litter they spot. Talk about natural versus human-produced litter. Leaves or weeds may be blowing in the school yard, but they are natural litter. Ask: How does the litter make the street look? How does litter make you feel?

C ▪ O ▪ N ▪ N ▪ E ▪ C ▪ T ▪ I ▪ O ▪ N ▪ S

To Language

Expressive Language - Children will describe their reactions to litter.

Science Concept

Many objects in our world have similar characteristics.

Science Process Skill

To focus observations by using the senses.

Science Vocabulary

dangerous

litter

safety

3. When you feel the children understand what litter is, take them on a litter-finding walk. Start this walk out with an introduction to safe litter pick up. Say: Be very careful of broken glass! And call me when you find a container that has something in it.

4. As the children walk, have them spot litter, identify it, and put it in a litter bag. Be sure to wash the children's hands after the activity.

5. Say: If you did a good job, you should now have a clean area.

6. Take another litter walk in a couple of days. Ask: What do you find that's new? How do you think the litter got there? How are the areas that are clean alike? What makes a clean place different from a place that is not clean?

7. Occasionally repeat the litter walk. If you find litter, talk about how important it is not to litter.

Observing the Children

Do the children recognize litter? Are they making any anti-littering comments?

ACTIVITY 2

Cloud Drawings

Materials

crayons or paints

paper

Clouds provide an excellent source of stimulation for children's drawing. An encyclopedia will tell you how to differentiate between cirrus, cumulus, and stratus clouds. What, for example, makes a cloud a cirrus? They are light and wispy. You can also have the children spot the thunderhead cloud, cumulonimbus.

C▪O▪N▪N▪E▪C▪T▪I▪O▪N▪S

To Language

Expressive Language - Children will use their own words to describe the clouds they see.

To Math

Comparing - Children will talk about large and small clouds.

Science Concept

Many objects in our world have different characteristics.

Science Process Skill

To focus observations by using the senses.

Science Vocabulary

cirrus

clouds

cumulus

day

night

sky

stratus

What to Do

1. Take the children outdoors. If the weather is not suitable, this activity can be done by looking out the window.

2. Have the children observe the clouds in the sky. You may want to lie on the ground to watch the clouds. Then, have the children draw or paint their interpretations. Do this over a period of time so they will be exposed to a variety of clouds and weather conditions. Talk about how clouds are alike and different.

3. If you want to introduce the cloud names, one way is to create a bulletin board with the three common cloud types. Some of the children may use the names of the clouds (cirrus, cumulus, stratus) when you supply the words. Ask: How are the clouds you see alike?

Observing the Children

The children's drawings should show an awareness that clouds are unique shapes in the sky. Do not look for realistic artwork, but for some pattern in their drawings and observations.

ACTIVITY 3

Do Dogs Talk?

Materials

dogs

paper and crayons (for a Discovery Book)

Dogs are in every community, and they afford us an easy opportunity to study animals in an outdoor setting. The children can observe and discuss how they behave and communicate with each other.

Before the Activity

Arrange to have one of the children bring a pet dog from home on the day of this activity.

What to Do

1. Talk about how we communicate with each other. Ask: How do you tell your family you are hungry? How do you ask a friend to share a toy with you? How do you let others know you are happy? Encourage the children to show each other what they do and say.

C ▪ O ▪ N ▪ N ▪ E ▪ C ▪ T ▪ I ▪ O ▪ N ▪ S

To Language

Expressive Language - Children will describe the dogs they see. Can they imitate the dog sounds they hear?

Discovery Book - Children will create captioned pictures of the dogs they observe.

To Math

Counting - Children will count the dogs they see on the walk.

Comparing - Children will use comparative language as they talk about the dogs they see.

Science Concept

Many objects in our world have different characteristics.

Science Process Skill

To focus observations by using the senses.

Science Vocabulary

animal

bark

breed

communicate

dog

dog names

whine

2. Have a child bring a pet dog from home to the classroom. Say: Let's watch (the dog's name) closely. Does the dog have ways to let us know how it is feeling? Are the ways that dogs communicate like the ways we communicate, or different?

3. Take the children for a walk in the neighborhood. Let the children watch more than one dog. Remind them to watch for the different ways dogs seems to be communicating to us and to each other. Say: We talk to each other. Do you think that dogs talk to each other? How?

4. After the walk, ask: How many dogs did you see on the walk? Did you see any of the same kind (breed) of dog? How many different dogs do you see?

5. Have the children draw pictures of the dogs they saw. Caption the pictures, and put them in a class Discovery Book.

Observing the Children

Do the children hypothesize about why dogs make sounds and move in certain ways?

ACTIVITY 4

The Great Tree Match

Materials

school yard or nearby park with at least three varieties of trees

collecting bags

a leaf from each of three varieties of trees (1 of each per bag)

Knowing the names of the trees in many school yards is fairly easy because few are planted. And knowing the names and the leaves of each of these trees gives the children a sense of knowledge about the outdoors that can lead to more exploration. We know that some trees have leaves that are alike, while others are very different.

Before the Activity

Collect leaves from each of the three trees. Place one of each type of leaf in each child's bag.

What to Do

1. Take the children on a leaf-collecting walk. Talk with the children about the shapes of the leaves as well as their colors and textures. Talk about the fact that a tree is a plant.

C▪O▪N▪N▪E▪C▪T▪I▪O▪N▪S

To Language

Expressive Language - Children will describe the shapes, textures, and colors of the leaves.

To Math

Matching - Children will find leaves to match the samples they have.

Classifying - Children will group the leaves.

Science Concept

Many objects in our world have similar characteristics.

Science Process Skill

To use observations to classify.

Science Vocabulary

bark

branches

leaf

roots

tree

tree names

trunk

veins

2. Hold up a pre-collected leaf and identify it. For example, if it is a maple leaf, say: This is a leaf from a maple tree. Let's see if we can find a maple tree. One way we can tell if it's a maple tree or not is by looking at its leaves. All of its leaves are alike.

3. Give a collecting bag to each child, and ask the children to look in their bags. Say: Three leaves are in your bag. I want you to take out a leaf that looks like the maple leaf I am holding.

4. When all the children have found the leaf, say: Let's try to find a maple leaf. Walk to the various trees and match the leaves until they find the proper match. The children will discover that each tree has its own special type of leaf, and that all leaves on a tree are usually alike.

5. Upon returning to the classroom, have the children group the leaves according to characteristics they choose.

Observing the Children

The children should choose leaves that are like those in their bags. Can they tell you why they grouped the leaves as they did? Did they use the words *alike* and *different* with their leaves?

ACTIVITY 5

School-Yard Rock Sorting

Materials

containers to hold rocks

extra rocks

crayons

Taking your children on a rock-collecting walk provides an opportunity for them to collect natural objects for which they can find important uses.

C ▪ O ▪ N ▪ N ▪ E ▪ C ▪ T ▪ I ▪ O ▪ N ▪ S

To Language

Expressive Language - Children will talk about the color, size, texture, and shape of their rocks.

To Math

Counting - Children will count the number of rocks in their collections.

Classifying - Children will find a number of ways to sort the rocks.

Comparing - Children will compare rock colors to crayon colors.

Science Concept

We can use the similarities and differences of objects to separate them into groups.

Science Process Skill

To use observations to classify.

Science Vocabulary

comparative terms such as small, long

geologist

rock

rock descriptors such as dull, rough

rock names

stone

What to Do

1. Take the children on a rock-collecting walk around the school yard. Tell them that *geologists* are people who work with rocks as their job. Some of the children may want to count the rocks they collect.

2. When they return to the classroom, let them sort their collected rocks by size.

3. Ask the children if they can suggest other ways to sort the rocks. Give them some help if necessary—they can sort by color, weight, shape, or texture. You may want to add extra rocks for increased variety. This is a good time to encourage the use of opposites such as *rough* and *smooth* or *shiny* and *dull*. Use comparative terms such as *large, medium, small, big, long,* and *widest.* Ask the children to tell how one rock is like or different from another.

4. Let the children match the colors of the rocks to the colors of their crayons.

Observing the Children

Can the children sort the rocks into piles by some criteria? Can they compare likes and differences? Can they match the color crayons to the rocks found?

ACTIVITY 6

Recycling

Materials

4 boxes to be used as recycling bins

litter bags

This activity is directly related to the recycling activities going on in many communities. The children will learn and practice good environmental skills while cleaning up litter.

What to Do

1. Ask the children if their families recycle at home. Some children may volunteer that they do. Ask them what kinds of things they recycle.

2. Ask: Where do you put things that are to be recycled? Do you have recycling bins at home? Say: I have brought some boxes to school. We can use them as recycling bins. If we go on a school-yard or neighborhood litter safari, what kinds of bins will we need? The children may say you will need bins for paper, aluminum, glass (some collection centers divide this into clear and colored glass), iron metal, and plastic (most collection centers restrict the type of plastic they will take). Discuss how the materials in the bins are alike and different.

C ▪ O ▪ N ▪ N ▪ E ▪ C ▪ T ▪ I ▪ O ▪ N ▪ S

To Language

Expressive Language - Children will talk about what is litter and what is not. Some may use their communication skills to talk about recycling in their homes.

To Math

Comparing - Children will talk about quantity using terms such as *more, most,* and *less.*

Counting - Children may count the items.

Science Concept

Many objects in our world have similar characteristics.

Science Process Skill

To use observations to classify.

Science Vocabulary

less, least

litter

names of categories

more, most

recycle

sort

3. Create four litter bins, label them, and take the class for a litter walk. Use the bags to collect litter. Some children may be able to count the items as they are collected.

4. When you have returned from the litter walk, let the children place the materials in the proper bins. Proper placement of some items will be difficult to determine, but will allow for lively discussions. Have the children compare the amount of litter in each bin. Ask: Which has more? Which has less?

Observing the Children

The children should be able to sort most of the materials into the proper bins. They should also be able to state how objects in the same bin are alike and how objects in different bins are different.

ACTIVITY 7

Pull a Weed

Materials

A weed is a plant that grows where we do not want it. Weeds are everywhere, and they can be used to show the different types of root systems. Tap roots, like carrots, are big, fleshy, and grow straight down. Diffused root systems, like grasses have, consist of small roots and rootlets that spread over a large area. The children do not need to know the names of the two groups, but this activity provides a unique way to observe and classify as well as a way to rid a vacant lot of weeds.

What to Do

1. Take the children on a walk to a vacant lot that is over-grown with weeds. **Caution:** Be aware of children who have allergies, and watch out for poison ivy, poison oak, sumac, and plants with spines.

C▪O▪N▪N▪E▪C▪T▪I▪O▪N▪S

To Language

Expressive Language - Children will describe how the two types of roots look different from each other. Also, encourage them to talk about the similarities and differences among the plants.

To Math

Comparing - Children will compare plants' root sizes and heights.

Counting - Children will count the number of plants in each group.

Classifying - Children will classify plants by type of root and may also classify them by size.

2. Ask the children to pull up some of the weeds and place them in a pile.

3. Let the children examine the weeds. Focus their attention on the plants' roots. Talk about characteristics of the roots, and help them compare root sizes and heights of plants. From their observations, help them find how roots are alike.

4. The children can sort and classify the weeds by their root systems, separating the weeds into two piles: those with tap roots and those with a diffused root system. Have them count the number of plants in each pile. Ask: How is a tap root different from a diffused root?

Observing the Children

Can the children identify the part of the plant that is the root? Can they tell why it is a root—that it is the part of the plant that grows in the ground? Can they point out how roots are alike?

Science Concept

We can use the similarities and differences of objects to separate them into groups.

Science Process Skill

To use observations to classify.

Science Vocabulary

diffused root system

flower

leaf

plant names

root, rootlets

soil

stem

tap root

weed

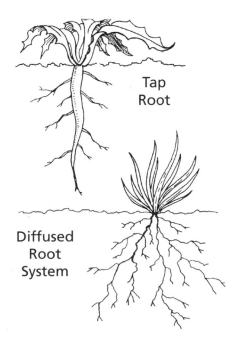

Tap Root

Diffused Root System

ACTIVITY 8

The Great Animal Search

Materials

plastic cups, some with lids and others without

large sheet of newsprint and markers (for a Discovery Chart)

colored markers

Finding animals in the yard is a worthwhile pursuit. Find, observe, and return will be the motto for this fun animal search. You will teach the children to collect but to not hurt. You can observe birds but cannot catch them. Squirrels' noisy antics can be observed, but you cannot capture one. They will eat a nut and leave the half-eaten shell. Insects can be caught, but they also leave cases and partially eaten leaves. Pieces of fur or feathers can be found on the ground, and spider webs hang down from branches.

What to Do

1. Talk about different animals and what might be found in the school yard. Talk about how you can tell if animals have been around.

2. Go to the nearest area where many different animals might be found, such as the school yard or the nearest park. Can the children find many animals that are alike, such as a flock of pigeons or a few squirrels?

C·O·N·N·E·C·T·I·O·N·S

To Language

Discovery Chart - You will make a chart to serve as a record of what was found (since everything will be returned to nature).

To Math

Classifying - Children may group common items before returning them. They may also compare the sizes of the groups.

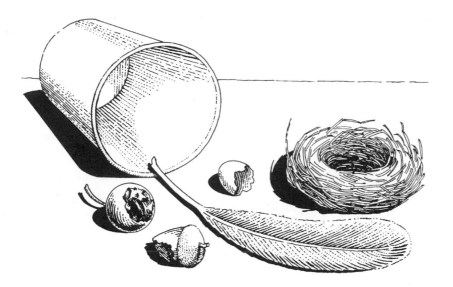

Science Concept

Many objects in our world have different characteristics.

Science Process Skill

To organize and communicate observations.

Science Vocabulary

animal names

evidence

nature

wildlife

3. Have the children look for animals. Show them evidence of animals that you find. Collect the animal or the evidence of its presence—a feather, a nut partially eaten, a broken egg, a fallen nest—and place it in a plastic cup. When a child makes a great find, observe and discuss what was found. Ask: What animal do you think left this evidence? Is it still around? Where? Observe the animal, if possible.

4. Bring some of the animals and evidence back to the center of the collection area. Talk with the children about what everyone has found. The children could group common items before returning them. They can also compare the sizes of the groups. Have the children return the animals and evidence to where they were found.

5. Make a Discovery Chart to help the children keep track of what they have found. Encourage the children to contribute their own information for the Discovery Chart, even if it is just a word or phrase.

6. Add to the chart in a different color when you repeat the activity.

Observing the Children

Do the children recognize the common animals in the park? Can they distinguish between the real thing and the evidence of the real thing's presence? Can they point out characteristics that make animals alike and that make them different?

ACTIVITY 9

Litter Graph

Materials

litter bags

large sheets of newsprint or tag board

glue

tape

This activity encourages the children to represent the materials they have been collecting in graphic form. From their graphs, some of the children may be able to visualize whether their efforts are really making a difference in litter removal. This activity could follow Going Outdoors Activity 1, Walk-Around-the-Block Litter Safari (page 86).

What to Do

1. Take the children on a collecting walk around the school yard, or use the materials you have collected during earlier walks. Encourage the children to talk about the things they find, as well as their feelings about littering.

2. After returning to the classroom, the children can make a litter graph on a large piece of newsprint or tag board. First have them sort the litter into groups—paper, plastic, metal, glass, and so on. Have them select several pieces of litter from each group.

C · O · N · N · E · C · T · I · O · N · S

To Language

Expressive Language - Children will talk about the things they find, as well as their feelings about littering. As they create the graph, they will use words such as *more, most,* and *the same as*.

To Math

Graphing - Children will create a graph of the litter they find.

Counting - Some of the children will be able to count the number of items in a column.

Science Concept

We can use the similarities and differences of objects to separate them into groups.

Science Process Skill

To organize and communicate observations.

Science Vocabulary

column

graph

litter

more, most

same as

3. Discuss how the materials in each group are alike but different from those in the other groups.

4. Give the children the newsprint or tag board. Show them how to glue or tape the items from each group into columns on the paper. Ask: Can you count the number of items in each group on your graph? As they create the graph, use words such as *more, most,* and *the same as.* If straight columns are a problem, guide the children as they place the objects in columns. Allow the glue to dry.

5. Display the litter graphs so you can discuss and count what has been collected. Saving the graphs can be one way to compare various weeks of litter information.

Observing the Children

The children should be able to recognize litter. Can they look at the graph and tell which column has the most items? Are they able to talk about how each column is alike or different from other columns?

UNIT 2

How Objects Move

Motion is one of the fundamental principles of the physical world. Only through an understanding of what motion is, what causes motion, and what alters motion can we begin to understand why objects in nature behave the way they do.

Motion is an important factor in a child's life almost from birth. As soon children start to wave their arms and legs, a natural fascination with movement begins. This unit is designed to help children understand more about the phenomenon of movement. They explore different aspects of movement, how motion can be controlled, and how movement affects them and their surroundings.

Organizing and Presenting the Unit

Phase 1: Free Discovery

Begin Free Discovery by talking with the children about how different things move and what we can do to make them move. Have some interesting things with you to show movement, such as a jack-in-the-box or a marble maze.

Ask the children to think of other things that move. Have them talk about how the things move.

As the children share their thoughts, encourage them to share their discoveries with you and add them to the How Objects Move Discovery Chart. You may also want to list all the ways they can think of to make their own bodies move.

Phase 2: Conducting the Activities

The second phase of Discovery Science takes place in your classroom learning centers (described in the section on the classroom centers). Use whatever approach to center management that you have found effective. The activities in this unit are general descriptions of developmentally appropriate activities for several traditional centers. Since the children will be varied in their level of cognitive development and physical maturity, offer a wide selection of activities. Choose the activities that are appropriate for your group.

Science Concepts

The following science concepts will be addressed in the How Objects Move Unit:

1. Motion occurs when force is applied to an object.

2. Changing the amount or direction of an applied force results in a change in motion.

3. In the everyday world, everything we observe moving eventually stops.

Getting Ready

Place the following materials in the Discovery Center for the children to explore during Free Discovery:

- objects that show movement, such as a jack-in-the-box or a marble maze

- large sheet of newsprint (for a Discovery Chart)

- markers

- marble and box

- assortment of hand-held fans, such as Chinese, paper, and pleated construction-paper fans

- things that will move air, like a dust pan

- air pump

- beach ball

- balloons

- children's spinning toys, such as tops

- toy cars

- plastic pipe 1 to 1.5 meters long and 5 centimeters in diameter

- elbow connector for 2-inch pipe

- tee connector for 2-inch pipe

- pieces of plastic foam insulated tubes, or cardboard tubes

Allow the children ample opportunities to investigate as many of the centers as possible, based on your time and space limitations. Some teacher assistance may be required to initiate the experience, but be careful not to over-direct the children.

Now is the time to initiate the class Discovery Books for this unit. You may want to use several books, each focused on a specific activity; a general book with drawings and captions showing what the children are learning about how objects move; or both.

As the children do the activities in the unit, add their discoveries to the How Objects Move Discovery Chart.

Phase 3: Making Connections to the Real World

The final phase of Discovery Science incorporates what the children have been experiencing in the classroom. In this phase, the children make discoveries about how the concept of motion is applied in the real world. These experiences will encourage the children to connect what they are learning in the classroom to adult roles and activities.

You may want to invite someone who uses moving objects in their occupation or hobby to share their knowledge and experience with the children. Perhaps someone could bring a sewing machine. A truck driver could show the children all the things that move on a truck.

Another useful idea is to take the children on a field trip to a location with a rich display of moving objects. This could be an automobile repair shop; a construction site with a bulldozer, cranes, and other equipment; or a car wash.

Language and Reading Center

Before you begin this unit, visit the library to select appropriate books and other resource materials to place in the Language and Reading Center. Posters and tapes will also add interest to the area, as will the display of Discovery Books, Discovery Charts, and other examples of the children's work during the unit. A number of books appropriate for this age level are listed here.

This Is the Way We Go to School by Edith Baer. New York: Scholastic, 1992.

This book shows the various modes of transportation young children all over the world use to get to school.

Feel the Wind by Arthur Dorros. New York: HarperCollins Children's Books, 1990.

The motion of air in the form of wind is discernible in many ways. Simple text accompanied by bright illustrations explains the causes, power, effects, and uses of wind. The book encourages outdoor exploration.

Gilberto and the Wind by Marie Hall Ets. New York: Puffin Books, 1963.

Gilberto, a very young boy, narrates this story about all the things he has experienced with wind. Some of the things he's done that involve the wind include losing his balloon, watching clothes flap on the line, blowing grass, flying his kite, and playing with his pinwheel.

So Can I by Margery Facklam. San Diego, Calif.: Gulliver Books/Harcourt, Brace, Jovanovich, 1988.

Each page in this book represents an animal in motion. Lift the flap to see a child moving the same way. Young readers are drawn to the repetitive language patterns and full-color watercolor illustrations.

On the Go by Ann Norris. New York: Lothrop, Lee and Shepard Books, 1990.

Excellent photographs and simple text show people from all over the world traveling on foot, in boats, on oxen backs, and in spaceships to move from place to place.

ACTIVITY 1

Track the Marble Roll

Materials

marbles

other objects that roll (optional)

tempera paint

shallow cups to hold paint

cardboard boxes

papers cut to the size of the box

paper towels (for clean up)

With a slow-motion camera you can take a series of pictures that show the motion or change of motion of a moving marble. Or, you can let the marble leave a track. The track method is easier to do in the early childhood classroom, because all you need is paint and a moveable object. The children will love the results.

What to Do

1. Show the children how to place a sheet of paper in the bottom of the cardboard box. Drop one marble in the box, and have the children watch it move around and change direction. Talk about how motion can be stopped and direction can be changed.

2. Tell them we want to make a picture that helps us remember what the marble did in the box as it moved. Dip a marble in the paint, and drop it in the box. Move the marble by moving the box until the marble stops leaving a track. Repeat with another color of paint to show the different tracks each marble took.

C ▪ O ▪ N ▪ N ▪ E ▪ C ▪ T ▪ I ▪ O ▪ N ▪ S

To Language

Expressive Language - Children will talk about the colorful trails left by the marbles.

To Math

Shapes - Children will identify the shapes created by the marble tracks.

Science Concept

Changing the amount or direction of an applied force results in a change in motion.

Science Process Skill

To focus observations by using the senses.

Science Vocabulary

across

curve

direction

motion words

stop

straight line

track

trail

3. Allow the children to show motion with marbles. When each child has finished a picture, hang them up to dry.

4. To extend this activity, give the children other objects that roll and see what kind of motion tracks they leave behind.

Observing the Children

Observe the children as they initiate this activity in groups or individually. Can they tell you where the marble changed direction in the picture?

One Moves Many

ACTIVITY 1

Materials

at least 10 rectangular blocks

Have you heard of the domino effect? Of course! The children, however, may not have experienced how one thing can move many things, as properly set-up dominoes can do. Dominoes or blocks allow children to experience multiple motion and chain reactions.

What to Do

1. Show the children how to arrange ten or more blocks in a line with a small space between each.

2. Have a child gently push the first block in the line toward the second block.

3. The first block will fall as the energy from the push to the first block is transferred from block to block. Have the children describe what must happen for all the blocks to fall.

C ▪ O ▪ N ▪ N ▪ E ▪ C ▪ T ▪ I ▪ O ▪ N ▪ S

To Language

Expressive Language - Children will describe what must happen for all the blocks to fall.

To Math

Counting and Patterning - Children will count the blocks they have set up. They will arrange blocks to establish patterns.

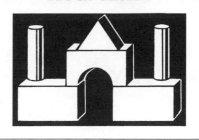

Science Concept

Motion occurs when force is applied to an object.

Science Process Skill

To focus observations by using the senses.

Science Vocabulary

fall

line

pattern

push

space

4. Repeat the activity, and have the children count the blocks they have set up. Then, just for fun, have them try to count the blocks as fast as they fall.

5. Let children set up the blocks in other configurations and let them fall where they may. Have them arrange the blocks to establish a pattern, such as big, little, big, little.

Observing the Children

Observe the children as they initiate this activity in groups or individually. Do they find other blocks or objects in the center that will work as well?

ACTIVITY 1

Little Red Wagon

Materials

child's wagon

blocks

Motion is everywhere, even in a little red wagon. The wagon is a useful vehicle that works because of the laws of motion. In this activity, the children will use a wagon to carry things and other children around the classroom. The more items in the wagon, the harder it is to set it in motion and to stop.

What to Do

1. Have the children take turns pushing each other in the wagon.

2. Start out with one child pulling one child. Then experiment with two children in the wagon and one child pulling. Then try three in the wagon and one pulling.

3. Try one child in the wagon and one, two, then three pulling.

C ▪ O ▪ N ▪ N ▪ E ▪ C ▪ T ▪ I ▪ O ▪ N ▪ S

To Language

Expressive Language - Children will discuss the difference between one person and two or more people pulling the wagon. They will talk about the difficulty of pulling an increasing number of people.

To Math

Counting and Graphing - Children will count the number of pushers and riders and represent them with stacks of blocks.

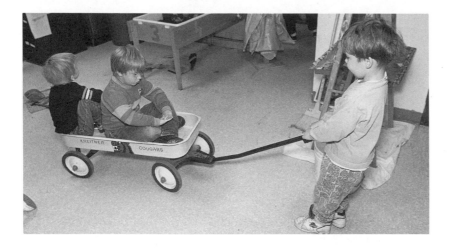

Science Concepts

Motion occurs when force is applied to an object.

Changing the amount or direction of an applied force results in a change in motion.

Science Process Skill

To focus observations by using the senses.

Science Vocabulary

hard, easy

push, pull

stop

4. Have the children start to keep track of how many children are being pulled by how many pullers by using the blocks. For example, if two children want to pull three children, have them pile up one pile of two blocks to represent the number of pullers, and a pile of three blocks to represent the riders.

5. For each combination of riders and pullers, discuss with the children how difficult the pulling was.

Observing the Children

Can the children tell you whether the wagon will be hard or easy to pull depending on the number of children in the wagon?

ACTIVITY 2

Shadow Dancing

Materials

white sheet

lamp

length of rope

music (optional)

Using a shadow on a sheet to observe a person's motion makes this activity fun and playful. This is the children's chance to play—and an opportunity for you to discuss and use some of the descriptive words about motion.

Before the Activity

Use the sheet and rope to create a curtain. Set up the sheet so that the lamp and at least two children can fit behind it.

C ▪ O ▪ N ▪ N ▪ E ▪ C ▪ T ▪ I ▪ O ▪ N ▪ S

To Language

Expressive Language - Children will describe the movement they observe as the shadows move before them.

To Math

Counting - Children will count the number of children doing certain motions.

Science Concept

Changing the amount or direction of an applied force results in a change in motion.

Science Process Skill

To focus observations by using the senses.

Science Vocabulary

directional terms such as up, down, right, left

move, movement

What to Do

1. Have the children sit in front of the sheet. Let them take turns going behind the sheet and moving. Can the other children describe the movements they see?

2. Have two or more children go behind the sheet. Let the other children count the number of children doing the same activity. For example, they might observe that one child is standing and two are jumping.

3. You might want to add music to this activity.

Observing the Children

The children should be able to observe the movement of a child's silhouette behind the screen and describe the way in which the child is moving.

ACTIVITY 1

Sailboat Races

Materials

pieces of plastic foam, wood, or other floating materials

scraps of thin plastic (plastic sheets or plastic lids) or index cards

craft sticks or nails to hold sails upright

scissors

water table or large, flat container filled with water

objects to create wind, such as fans and air pumps

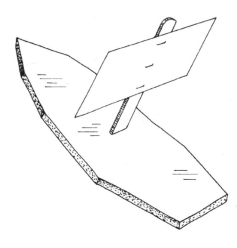

With a water table and some lung power, you can introduce the world of pretend sailboats and wind-powered machines. In this activity, you will create a model boat and show how wind power can move objects across water. Children will explore whether some objects move better with the wind than others.

Before the Activity

Gather enough materials that children can be creative when building their boats. Use the materials to create a model boat. Make several boats ahead of time if you have children who may have difficulty creating a boat themselves.

What to Do

1. Show children how they can fashion a sailboat from the variety of materials. The children may need some help with this, and your model may serve to simplify the process. These do not have to be works of art. They just need to float.

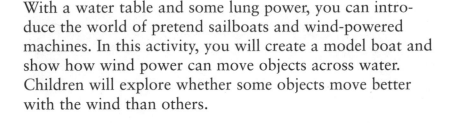

C ▪ O ▪ N ▪ N ▪ E ▪ C ▪ T ▪ I ▪ O ▪ N ▪ S

To Language

Expressive Language - Children will share their excitement with each other using words such as faster, fastest, and slow.

To Math

Sequencing - Children may group the boats in order of sailing ability.

Science Concepts

Motion occurs when force is applied to an object.

Changing the amount or direction of an applied force results in a change in motion.

Science Process Skill

To focus observations by using the senses.

Science Vocabulary

across

air pump

blow

fan

float

move

sail

sideways

wind

2. Demonstrate how they can blow on a sailboat and cause it to move across the simulated lake.

3. Encourage the children to try blowing together on one boat or to try blowing sideways. Ask one child to blow from one direction and another from the opposite direction. Have them try different objects, such as fans and air pumps, to move the boats.

4. Talk with the children about why the boats are moving and what happens when they try different ways to push the boat.

5. Have the children group the boats in order of their ability to sail, from good to not as good (optional).

Observing the Children

Watch to see if the children have any idea of where their boats will go according to the direction they are blowing. If more than one child is working to make the boat move faster or for a longer distance, it is an indication that they understand that the force of their blowing is causing the boats to move across the water. Do they understand that by pooling their efforts they can apply more force?

ACTIVITY 2

Paddle Boat Races

Materials

variety of plastic foam pieces suitable for shaping into boats and paddles

several pairs of scissors

assortment of rubber bands

duct tape

water table or large, flat container filled with water

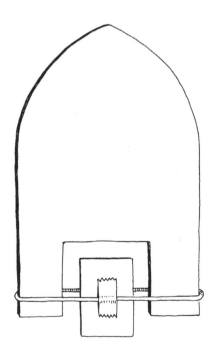

Once the children have mastered the wind-powered boat, move to the powered boat. Some families may be able to lend powered boats. They are also available in toy and hobby stores. The illustrations will show you how to create a simple power boat with a rubber-band drive.

Before the Activity

Make a model boat using the materials. Make several boats ahead of time if you have children who may have difficulty creating a boat.

What to Do

1. Talk with the children about what they know about boats and how they might build one from the plastic foam pieces.

2. Have the children design their own boats. The overall design is not important, but you will have to provide some guidance when it comes to making the propelling device. The propeller must resemble a paddle wheel. It is attached to the main part of the boat by the rubber band. Refer to diagrams for a basic design of the paddle boat. Once again, this will require some assistance on your part and a model boat will speed the process. For the younger children, use the preconstructed boats.

C▪O▪N▪N▪E▪C▪T▪I▪O▪N▪S

To Language

Expressive Language - Children will have much to discuss about how their paddle boat was made and how it performs.

Science Concepts

Changing the amount or direction of an applied force results in a change of motion.

In the everyday world, everything we observe moving eventually stops.

Science Process Skill

To focus observations by using the senses.

Science Vocabulary

boat

farther

faster

forward

movement words

paddle

propel, propeller

3. Allow the children to experiment with their paddle boats to discover how they work. Eventually, share with them how to tape the paddle to the boat and then wind the rubber band to propel the boat through the water. Encourage the children to use words that describe the boat's movement, for example, *straight, circles,* and *loopy.*

4. Talk about how to make the boats go farther or faster.

Observing the Children

Watch to see if the children understand the relationship between winding the rubber band and the movement of the boat. Do they understand that by winding the rubber band tighter, the boats go farther and faster? Do they know what happens to the boat when the rubber band is completely unwound?

ACTIVITY 3

Bobbers and Bottomers

Materials

water table or large, flat container filled with water

variety of objects that will sink or float

paper towels (for clean up)

This activity is a new twist to an old concept frequently introduced to young learners: sink and float. This time, instead of placing all objects on the water surface and observing whether they sink or float, children will hold objects down on the bottom of the water container and release them. The "bobbers" will float to the surface and the "bottomers" will stay on the bottom.

What to Do

1. Show the children how to hold objects on the bottom of the water container. Select a bobber and a bottomer, and hold one down with each hand. While children are watching, release both objects.

2. Point to the floating object and call it a "bobber." Point to the object remaining on the bottom and call it a "bottomer."

C ▪ O ▪ N ▪ N ▪ E ▪ C ▪ T ▪ I ▪ O ▪ N ▪ S

To Language

Expressive Language - Children will use related vocabulary to explain whether their object is a bobber or a bottomer.

To Math

Grouping - Children will be asked to create two sets of objects—those that bob to the surface and those that stay underwater.

Counting - Children will count the number of bobbers and bottomers they have discovered.

Science Concept

Motion occurs when force is applied to an object.

Science Process Skill

To use observations to classify.

Science Vocabulary

bobber, bob

bottom

heavy, light

sink, float

3. Ask a child to select an object, hold it on the bottom of the tub, and then let it go.

4. Have that child or any of the others tell you whether the object is a bobber or bottomer.

5. Continue this process with several children until you have several bobbers and bottomers identified. Count them, put them into two groups, and make labels for the groups.

6. Leave the rest of the objects and the tub of water at the Sand and Water Center. Encourage children to continue to investigate which objects are bobbers and bottomers and to place them in their appropriate group.

Observing the Children

Observe the accuracy with which children place their objects in groups. While they are holding objects down, ask them to predict whether the objects are going to stay on the bottom or bob to the top. If the children have been investigating the principle of buoyancy, they will have come to associate the upward push from the object as a predictor of floating.

ACTIVITY 1

Balloon Pendulum

Materials

large, inflated balloon

string

air pump

assortment of fans

assortment of objects that do not move air significantly, such as string and a toothbrush

In this activity, an inflated balloon hanging from the classroom ceiling captures children's imaginations and attention. It becomes an object to be set in motion as children experiment with ways of making the balloon move.

What to Do

1. Suspend the inflated balloon by the string from the ceiling in an open location.

2. Gather children around the balloon. Generate ideas from them on how to make the balloon move without touching it. Show them the materials you have collected that might be used to make the balloon move. Encourage them to try to make the balloon move using the objects.

3. Now talk with them about how to make the balloon move farther, faster, or in a different direction. Let them experiment and see what they can do.

C•O•N•N•E•C•T•I•O•N•S

To Language

Expressive Language - Children will name all the objects that were or were not able to move the balloon.

To Math

Grouping - Children may group the objects by ability to make the balloon move.

Science Concepts

Motion occurs when force is applied to an object.

In the everyday world, everything we observe moving eventually stops.

Science Process Skill

To focus observations by using the senses.

Science Vocabulary

balloon

direction

fan

farther

faster

move

wind

4. Ask: What happens to the balloon if we stop trying to move it?

5. The children can place all the objects that made the balloon move in one group and those that do not in another group (optional).

Observing the Children

The children should use the process of trial and error to initially determine how they can make the balloon move. Eventually, you should observe them selecting objects that will really make the balloon move around.

ACTIVITY 2

The Rolling Beach Ball

With a beach ball you can experiment with the concept that motion occurs when a force is applied. Encourage the children to be resourceful and creative as they find new ways to make the ball move by applying different kinds of force.

Materials

large, inflated beach ball

assortment of devices to make the ball move, such as an air pump, a plastic bat, and a fan

What to Do

1. Place the beach ball in the center of the room. Talk with the children about how they can move the ball, move it in different directions, and make it stop moving.

2. Ask one child to come forward, select a means of moving the ball, and then try the method. Discuss with the child what has just happened and why the ball moved.

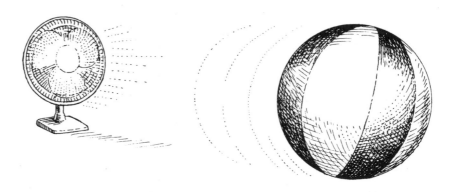

C ▪ O ▪ N ▪ N ▪ E ▪ C ▪ T ▪ I ▪ O ▪ N ▪ S

To Language

Expressive Language - The children will orally predict the direction and distance the ball will move.

Science Concepts

Motion occurs when force is applied to an object.

Changing the amount or direction of an applied force results in a change in motion.

Science Process Skill

To focus observations by using the senses.

Science Vocabulary

direction

force

stop

3. Have another child select a new way of moving the ball. Can the children guess which way the ball will move when the force is applied?

4. Repeat this activity, always encouraging the children to think of new ways to move the ball.

Observing the Children

The children should be able to select objects that will move the ball easily and predict the direction the ball will move.

ACTIVITY 3

Four Square

When the children have learned enough about stopping, starting, and changing an object's motion, it is time to test their skill. This activity checks out whether the children can apply their knowledge to cause a balloon to hit inside a square. Because this activity may be more fun than easy, it may take time.

Materials

large, inflated balloon

4 air-moving devices, such as air pumps, fans, pieces of cardboard, or waving hands

chalk, or posterboard and marker

What to Do

1. Use chalk or poster board and marker to draw a large square on top of a table or in the center of the room on the floor. Divide the square into four equal squares.

2. Select four children to position themselves at the outside corner of each of the squares. Give each one an air-moving device (waving hands can be one of the methods).

3. Instruct the children to try to move the balloon to different squares by using only their air-moving devices.

C▪O▪N▪N▪E▪C▪T▪I▪O▪N▪S

To Language

Expressive Language - Children will predict whether they will be moving the balloon to the square at their right, left, or across from them.

To Math

Numeral Recognition - Children will identify the numbers of the squares.

Science Concepts

Changing the amount or direction of an applied force results in a change in motion.

Motion occurs when force is applied to an object.

Science Process Skill

To focus observations by using the senses.

Science Vocabulary

across

push

right, left

square

wave

wind

4. Talk with the children about which square they are trying to move the balloon to. Challenge them to move the balloon to a particular square.

5. As a variation, you can number the four squares and talk with the children about which square their balloon is in and which they will attempt to move it to.

Observing the Children

Watch to see if the children are able to move the balloon in the direction they choose. Observe whether they understand that the direction they pump the air influences how the balloon moves.

ACTIVITY 4

The Motion Machine

Materials

record player

box or circular pan

marble or small ball

objects to place on the turntable, such as blocks, paper clips, small rocks, and plastic chips

paper plates

colored markers

The motion machine is made from an old record player that still has a motor to do a little work for the children. The centrifugal force of the rotating turntable will cause objects to move to the outside. At low speeds the movement will be gradual. At high speeds it will be immediate, and even flat blocks might move to the outside. This is a nice way to give new life to an old piece of equipment.

Before the Activity

Make a motion machine. Put a hole in the bottom of the box or pan, and place it on the center of the turntable. Experiment with the speed of the record player until the box stays in place.

What to Do

1. Place the motion machine in the Discovery Center. Let one child place a marble or ball in the machine. (The most action occurs when the object is placed in the center.) Talk with the children about what they think will happen when the machine is set into motion. Turn the machine on and watch.

2. Talk about what happened. Did the ball roll or stay still? Where and how did it roll? Now remove the ball.

C ▪ O ▪ N ▪ N ▪ E ▪ C ▪ T ▪ I ▪ O ▪ N ▪ S

To Language

Written - The children can draw their observations. They might also dictate labels for the unique artwork created when the objects are dipped in paint and spun on the motion machine.

Science Concepts

Motion occurs when force is applied to an object.

Changing the amount or direction of an applied force results in a change in motion

Science Process Skill

To focus observations by using the senses.

Science Vocabulary

center

fast, faster

machine

motion

movement

rotate

roll

slow, slower

still

turn

3. Have another child select a different object and place it in the machine. Compare the results. Have the children experiment by putting objects in different places and by choosing different objects to be set into motion in the motion machine. Ask: Does the speed at which the turntable moves affect the movement of the objects?

4. Put a paper plate on the motion machine by pushing a hole up through the center of the plate. Show the children how they can hold a marker on the plate as the turntable turns to create different patterns. Try different color combinations.

5. Leave the machine in the center. Encourage the children to share any new discoveries.

Observing the Children

Watch for evidence of understanding of cause and effect on the part of the children. Do they know that the object will move differently when put in different places?

ACTIVITY 5

Spinning Tops

Materials

several tops

variety of objects similar to tops that may or may not truly spin like a top, such as gyroscopes, marbles, flat spinning discs, jacks, and balls

2 boxes

The toy top is an excellent model of motion that results from the application of force. Other objects can also spin. This activity lets the children observe motion in action—not only with tops, but with other common objects as well.

What to Do

1. Demonstrate how to make one of the tops spin. Give children an opportunity to investigate how they can make the top spin as you have done. Talk about how the children's energy can be used to spin the top faster or slower.

2. Now make all the tops and other objects available to them. Allow the children to experiment and to discover which objects are "good" spinners and which are not. (Good spinners are those that make several revolutions. You may have to help the children establish criteria for good spinners.)

C ▪ O ▪ N ▪ N ▪ E ▪ C ▪ T ▪ I ▪ O ▪ N ▪ S

To Language

Expressive Language - Children will use words and comparisons to describe the differences in the objects that spin or do not spin, such as *twirl, whirl, fast,* and *crooked.*

To Math

Grouping - Children will classify objects as those that are good spinners and those that are not.

Science Concepts

Motion occurs when force is applied to an object.

Changing the amount or direction of an applied force results in a change in motion.

Science Process Skill

To use observations to classify.

Science Vocabulary

move

spin

top

3. Set out the two boxes. Ask the children to place objects that are good spinners in one box and those that aren't in the other box.

Observing the Children

Can the children place the investigated objects into the appropriate groups based on their definition of a good spinner?

ACTIVITY 6

What Rolls?

Materials

variety of objects, some that roll and some that do not, such as toy cars, balls, and blocks

blocks, books, or other materials to make ramps

Children witness motion every day. In fact, children themselves are excellent examples of motion in action. This activity lets them observe and predict items they think will roll or not roll. As a final exercise, the children get into the act.

What to Do

1. Talk with the children about what we mean when we say an object *rolls*. Show them several objects that roll, and demonstrate what rolling means. Ask if they can think of other things that roll.

2. Let the children investigate whether or not the objects you have selected for them will roll.

3. Have the children explore around the room to see if they can find other objects they think might roll and try them.

C·O·N·N·E·C·T·I·O·N·S

To Language

Expressive Language - Children will use their expressive language skills as they share their ideas of things they think can roll.

To Math

Classification - Children will sort objects into two groups and classify them as rollers or nonrollers.

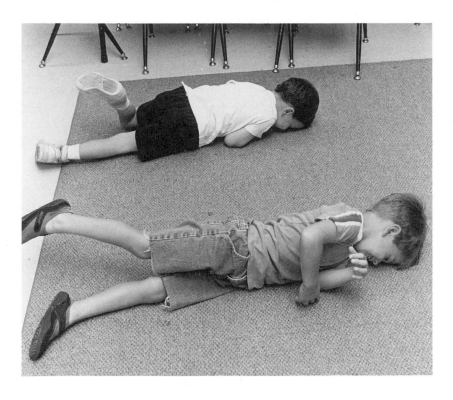

Science Concept

Motion occurs when force is applied to an object.

Science Process Skill

To use observations to classify.

Science Vocabulary

move

pull

push

roll

wheels

4. Have the children place the objects that roll in one location and the objects that do not roll in another. Talk with them about why some objects roll and some do not roll.

5. Finish the discussion by asking the children if they can roll. Show them how to do body rolls, and suggest that they pretend they are wheels that roll across the room.

6. Send home How Objects Move Family Connection Activity 1 (page 335).

Observing the Children

Can the children correctly classify the objects?

ACTIVITY 7

Turn Right, Turn Left

Materials

piece of plastic pipe 5 centimeters in diameter and 1 to 1.5 meters long (3 to 4 feet)

1 elbow connector

1 tee connector

several small marbles or rubber balls

2 boxes

This activity puts the children into the action as they observe and then experiment with movement control. They will enjoy using balls in this new way.

What to Do

1. Show the children how to arrange the boxes about 60 centimeters (a few feet) apart with the open sides facing each other. Put the elbow connector on a piece of pipe.

2. Show the children how they can lay the elbow end of the pipe on the floor between the two boxes and hold the other end in their hands so that when they release a ball, it rolls down the pipe. Ask: How many objects do you think will roll into the boxes?

C·O·N·N·E·C·T·I·O·N·S

To Language

Expressive Language - Discussion will focus on the effect of pipe angle and various connectors on the accuracy of the rolling balls.

To Math

Counting and Estimating - Children will estimate how many balls will roll into the boxes. Then they will count the balls that hit the target and those that missed the boxes.

Science Concept

Changing the amount or direction of an applied force results in a change in motion.

Science Process Skill

To use observations to classify.

Science Vocabulary

control

move

pipe

release

roll

turn

3. Let them experiment with rolling the balls and trying to get one in a box.

4. After they have had experience with the elbow, give them the tee connector. Let them discover the difference in the predictability of the outcome.

5. Have the children count the number objects that roll into a box and the number that miss the box.

Observing the Children

Do the children understand that they can control the direction in which the ball will roll when they use the elbow connector and that it is much more difficult to influence the outcome with the tee connector?

ACTIVITY 8

Things That Bounce

Materials

variety of objects, some that bounce and some that will not

From infancy, children enjoy watching things that bounce. Although they see other items that have this characteristic, their responses to something that bounces is usually "a ball." This activity lets the children explore and investigate many things in their world that bounce.

Before the Activity

Gather several bouncing and nonbouncing objects. Select a few bouncing objects that are not shaped like balls so the children can observe that not all objects that bounce are balls. Make sure there are plenty of objects in the room that the children can collect for the bounce test.

What to Do

1. Start this activity with a discussion of what it means to bounce. Demonstrate with an item from your collection. Show the children how *they* can bounce by jumping up and down in place.

C • O • N • N • E • C • T • I • O • N • S

To Language

Expressive Language - Children will talk about the objects they know will bounce and objects they think will bounce. Encourage the children to explain why they made a certain decision.

To Math

Sorting - Children will sort objects into two groups— those that bounce and those that will not bounce.

DISCOVERY CENTER

Science Concepts

Motion occurs when force is applied to an object.

In the everyday world, everything we observe moving eventually stops.

Science Process Skill

To use observations to classify.

Science Vocabulary

bounce

find

test

up, down

2. Bring out the other objects you have selected. Show the children how some objects bounce when they are dropped and how other objects just stop when they hit the ground. Let the children try bouncing the various objects.

3. Have the children search the room for objects that they predict might be bouncers. As they find objects, have them bring them to the group for investigating.

4. Let each child take a turn testing an object. Have the children place objects that bounce in one pile and place those that do not in another pile.

Observing the Children

Are the children sorting objects into correct groups? Do they have some ability to predict, in advance of dropping the objects, whether they will indeed bounce?

ACTIVITY 9

Balloon Power

Materials

variety of objects, some that can roll easily, such as toy cars, and some that cannot, such as blocks

tape

several balloons in different sizes

Balloons can be used to show how work can be done by one object acting on another. In this activity, an inflated balloon is taped to an object, and the object moves across the floor as the children watch. They will be delighted with their task: Which balloons move which objects, and how much do they move them?

What to Do

1. Blow up one of the larger balloons and tie it closed. Ask: What will happen if I let go of the balloon? Let it go and discuss how it is moving.

2. Blow up another large balloon, but this time do not tie it closed. Ask: What will happen if I let go of this balloon? Let it go. Talk about how this balloon moved differently from the balloon that was tied.

3. Select one of the toy cars or other rolling objects. Blow up the large balloon again, and use a long piece of tape to fasten the inflated balloon to the object without

C ▪ O ▪ N ▪ N ▪ E ▪ C ▪ T ▪ I ▪ O ▪ N ▪ S

To Language

Expressive Language - Children will verbalize their excitement as the balloons are released. Descriptors of movement and distance moved will prevail.

To Math

Counting - Children will count objects that moved and those that did not move. They will sort and classify movers and nonmovers.

Science Concept

Motion occurs when force is applied to an object.

Science Process Skill

To use observations to classify.

Science Vocabulary

air

big, little

blow

experiment

group

heavy, light

move

movement

separate

size

sort

releasing any air. Discuss with the children what will happen when the object is placed on the floor and the balloon is let free. Release the balloon. Talk about how the object moved across the floor.

4. Have the children select objects to attach to inflated balloons. Have them investigate which objects the balloons can move and which objects it cannot move. Balloons placed just any way will not cause an object to move. They will have to experiment with the balloon's location on an object to get maximum (or any) movement. Try different sizes of balloons.

5. Have the children sort the objects by those the balloon moved and those it did not move. Ask: Can you count the number in each pile?

Observing the Children

Can the children recognize that some objects will move easily with the balloon and others will not? They should be able to put the balloon on rolling objects so the objects move. A car will move when the balloon is placed correctly; the children should be able to say this and make some guesses on newly introduced objects.

ACTIVITY 10

Rocket on a String

Materials

10-meter piece of string

several balloons in different sizes and shapes

tape

soda straw

2 chairs

This balloon activity is in most aerospace and physics books to show action and reaction. When the air escapes the end of the balloon, it forces the straw to move forward on the string. The children can see the rocket moving and can talk about how much air you had to blow into the balloon before it would move a certain distance. Sometimes the rocket will zip across the entire length of the room or climb three stories up a string. Practicing and placing the balloon on the string properly is the secret to reaching those lofty or lengthy goals.

Before the Activity

Cut approximately 5 centimeters of straw and thread it through the string. Tie both ends of the string to the backs of two chairs. Pull the chairs apart to make the string taut.

C·O·N·N·E·C·T·I·O·N·S

To Language

Expressive Language - Children will use descriptors to describe the movement of the straw on the string.

To Math

Measuring - Children will learn how to measure the distance the straw traveled by using a nonstandard unit of length.

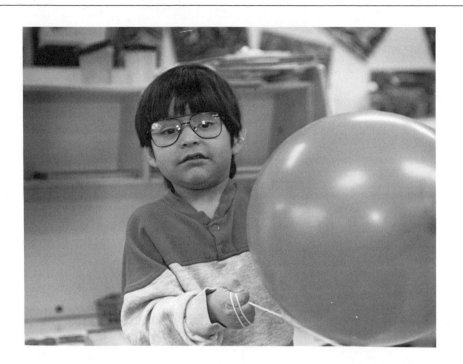

Science Concepts

Motion occurs when force is applied to an object.

Changing the amount or direction of an applied force results in a change in motion.

Science Process Skill

To organize and communicate observations.

Science Vocabulary

air

blow

distance

farther, shorter

inflate

move

What to Do

1. Blow up one of the balloons. Discuss with the children what will happen if the balloon is released.

2. Tape the inflated, untied balloon to the straw on the string. Pull the straw to one end of the string. Discuss with the children what will happen if you release the balloon now. Let it go, and talk about what you observe.

3. Repeat the process with a variety of balloons, always discussing with the children what they observe.

4. Keep a record of which balloons went the farthest by laying them on the ground under the string at the distance they traveled on the string.

5. Continue to refer to the continuum of balloons on the ground. Ask: Did this balloon go farther than this one? How do you know?

Observing the Children

Can the children give reasons for why some of the balloons go farther on the string? Do they state that more air in the balloon will make it go farther and relate this to blowing the balloon up bigger?

ACTIVITY 11

Swing High, Swing Low

Materials

plastic bucket

heavy string

variety of objects with different masses, such as blocks, toys, balls, pieces of plastic foam, and shoes

This activity introduces children to the concept of the pendulum. The children will discover that the more mass in the bucket, the more force they need to stop or start it.

What to Do

1. Tie the bucket to the string. Suspend it in the center of the room.

2. Ask the children to stand in a circle around the bucket. **Caution:** Be very careful with the placement of the children in the circle, because the bucket can come back hard and hit a child in the face. To determine how far away from the hanging bucket the children should stand, first swing the bucket hard. Then place the children in a circle at the edge of the circumference of the arc that the bucket made.

C▪O▪N▪N▪E▪C▪T▪I▪O▪N▪S

To Language

Expressive Language - Children will use the comparative terms *heavier* and *lighter* as they observe and feel the effects of weight on motion.

To Math

Counting - Children will count the objects in the bucket as the activity begins. They will continue to add to the count as objects are placed in the bucket.

Science Concepts

Motion occurs when force is applied to an object.

In the everyday world, everything we observe moving eventually stops.

Science Process Skill

To organize and communicate observations.

Science Vocabulary

catch

easy, hard

full, empty

heavy, heavier

light, lighter

motion words

push

stop

swing

3. Begin pushing the bucket to different children in the circle. Talk with them about how hard it is to stop the bucket when it comes to them. Have them push the bucket to someone else. Discuss how hard it is to push the bucket.

4. Put an object inside the bucket. Continue to pass the bucket back and forth around the group, always talking about how hard it is to stop and start the swinging bucket.

5. Put a heavier object inside the bucket. Have the children compare catching and pushing the bucket with the new object in the box.

6. Ask: Is the bucket hardest to push when it is full or empty? When is it easiest to push? Continue to change the objects in the bucket. Let the children take turns orally identifying heavy and light loads.

Observing the Children

Can the children use motion words as they identify the easiest and hardest loads to stop (catch)?

ACTIVITY 1

How Far Can You Jump?

Materials

masking tape

string in 2 different colors

scissors

A child who is in good physical shape should be able to jump from a standing position a distance equal to his or her height. A standing jump takes a lot of energy, and a child can jump just so far. But when a child runs, or adds the energy of running (force), he or she can jump much farther. Olympic jumpers use their knowledge of physics to improve their jumps.

What to Do

1. Place a short piece of masking tape on the floor. Talk to the children about jumping. Say: Can you jump? Show me! How far can you jump? Let's find out. We can use this string to measure our jumping distance.

2. Have a child place both feet at the tape mark and jump from a standing start. Use one color of string to measure the child's standing jump distance. Cut the length of string and give it to the child. Repeat for each of the children.

C•O•N•N•E•C•T•I•O•N•S

To Language

Expressive Language - Children will talk about how, and how far, they can jump.

To Math

Measuring - Children will learn how to measure their jumps using a nonstandard unit of measurement.

Comparing - Children will compare lengths of jumps by standing and running starts.

Science Concept

Changing the amount or direction of an applied force results in a change in motion

Science Process Skill

To focus observations by using the senses.

Science Vocabulary

compare

far, farther, farthest

force

graph

jump

measure

motion

move

run

start

3. Repeat the procedure, only this time let the children have a running start of 1.5 to 2 meters (4 to 6 feet). (**Caution:** A child may have problems with falling when too much force is applied in a jump.) Measure their jump distance using the second string color, and give the measurement string to the children.

4. The children can now compare the measurement strings from their standing jump and their running jump. Ask: Which jump was the farthest? What do you think helped you to jump farther?

5. Allow the children to compare their strings of the same color with each other.

6. Send home How Objects Move Family Connection Activity 2 (page 335).

Observing the Children

Listen to the children's comments as they compare their standing jump to their running jump. Determine if they conceptualize the significance of the difference between the two colors of string—one is the length of a standing jump, and the other is the length of a running jump. Do they relate greater strength used in the jump as greater force? Does greater force equal greater distance? Does greater force make stopping more difficult?

ACTIVITY 2

Can You Move Me?

Materials

scooter boards or some similar device

The relationship between the amount of mass and the force needed to move that mass is explored here in a fun and exciting way. A certain amount of force is needed to push a child sitting on a scooter board. More force is required to push two children—or one teacher—on the scooter board. How much force can be calculated in a formula, but you can leave that concept for later. Right now, more push for more mass is the concept.

What to Do

1. Sit on the scooter board in the middle of the classroom. Ask the children: Why am I not moving? Can you help me move? What can you do to make me move?

2. Let the children try to move you.

3. Now ask the children if they can help you stop moving. Move, and let them try to stop you. Talk with them about what happens when they try to stop you. Ask: Can you feel the scooter pushing you?

C▪O▪N▪N▪E▪C▪T▪I▪O▪N▪S

To Language

Expressive Language - Children will talk about movement and how they can cause it as well as stop it.

To Math

Counting - Children will count how many children it takes to move the teacher on the scooter board.

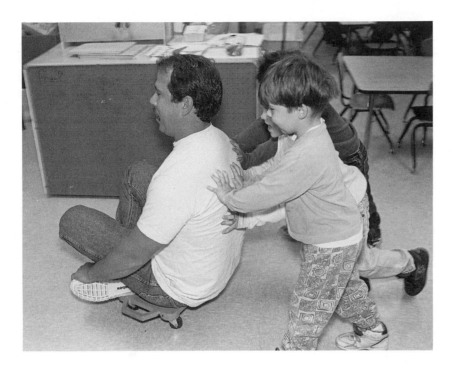

Science Concepts

Changing the amount or direction of an applied force results in a change in motion.

In the everyday world, everything we observe moving eventually stops.

Science Process Skill

To focus observations by using the senses.

Science Vocabulary

move

pull

push

stop

4. Have the children take turns pushing you on the scooter board. Ask: How many children does it take to move me?

5. Divide the children into pairs. Have them take turns pushing and stopping each other on the scooter boards.

Observing the Children

Observe pairs as they work together pushing and stopping each other. Ask the children to tell you what their roles are. Are they pushing the scooter (making it move) or stopping the scooter?

ACTIVITY 3

Eight Ball in the Corner Pocket

Bank a ball off the edge of a sidewalk in miniature golf or bounce a basketball off the floor, and the rules of motion come into play. Understanding how objects move as they change direction will be important when your young scientists become astrophysicists. For now, knowing something about the change in direction of a moving object can be fascinating and useful.

Materials

plastic foam rods or wrapping-paper tubes

tennis balls, wooden cubes, and other items that will roll, slide, or skip when pushed

snack-chip cans or small blocks

Before the Activity

Make soft "pool cues" out of lengths of plastic foam or by putting tape over the ends of wrapping-paper tubes.

What to Do

1. Set aside a playing field. Stand the snack-chip can upright in the center of the field, or build towers of small blocks.

C▪O▪N▪N▪E▪C▪T▪I▪O▪N▪S

To Language

Expressive Language - Children will use descriptive language as they talk about objects that move freely and those that do not.

To Math

Counting - Children will count the number of times they successfully knock down the piles of blocks or the can.

Classifying - Children will sort or classify objects that are efficient pool balls and those that are not.

Science Concept

Changing the amount or direction of an applied force results in a change in motion.

Science Process Skill

To focus observations by using the senses.

Science Vocabulary

direction

move

push

roll

skip

slide

2. Demonstrate to the children how they can use the tube as a cue stick to shoot the tennis ball at the target, trying to knock it down.

3. Let the children try it. They may need a little help from you, especially if they are younger children.

4. Replace the tennis ball with a variety of objects. Let the children see if the objects will knock down the target. Have the children count the number of times they knock it down.

5. Have the children keep those objects that knock down the target separate from those that do not work. Ask them to compare how well each item worked.

6. Talk with the children about why some objects make better pool balls than other objects.

Observing the Children

As the children play the game, do they consistently choose objects that serve as effective pool balls?

ACTIVITY 4

Freeze!

Materials

large red paper circle

large green paper circle

Our bodies move in many ways. We run, walk, crawl, and even roll to move. Action is complex, and it is often necessary to create rules for when motion can take place. You can move (cross) on a green light, but you should stop on a red light. The faster you are moving when you reach a red light, the more energy you will need to stop. The children can apply their information about movement to a new situation: when and when not to move.

What to Do

1. Have the children line up across the room from you.

2. Tell them when you hold up the green light, they can start moving toward you. When you hold up the red light, they must stop immediately, or "freeze."

3. Hold up the green circle, then the red circle. As you alternate back and forth between the two circles, talk with the children about their movement. Ask: What do you have to do to stop? What happens if you try to stop too suddenly? Can you start real fast?

4. Turn the activity into a language game with one of the children calling out the green and red sequence.

C ▪ O ▪ N ▪ N ▪ E ▪ C ▪ T ▪ I ▪ O ▪ N ▪ S

To Language

Expressive Language - Children will share information about motion behaviors that occur when they see red and green lights.

SMALL GROUP

Science Concept

In the everyday world, everything we observe moving eventually stops.

Science Process Skill

To focus observations by using the senses.

Science Vocabulary

freeze

go

start

stop

Observing the Children

Look for children that can follow the commands correctly. When it is their turn to call for red and green circles, do they know what will result with the color they have selected? Can they relate street light colors to movement activities?

ACTIVITY 5

Slower, Slower, Stop!

Materials

piece of chalk

at least 2 large, rubber balls

large sheets of red paper

Movement and moving objects interest most children. Activities in which children get to see objects fly or float about create enthusiastic responses. Because of the basic laws of motion, most movement eventually ends. With this activity, the cessation of movement becomes the focus of interest.

Before the Activity

Cut octagons out of the red paper. Print the word STOP in the middle of each to resemble stop signs.

What to Do

1. Take the children to a large open area, such as the gym or a hallway.

2. At one end of the space, use the chalk to draw a large circle (5 meters or more in diameter) on the floor.

3. Move to the other end of the area. Demonstrate to the children how to carefully give the ball a push and let it roll down the floor until it slowly comes to rest in the circle.

C·O·N·N·E·C·T·I·O·N·S

To Language

Expressive Language - Children will share their ideas about how to make the ball roll farther or less far.

To Math

Counting - Children will count the number of tries needed to roll the ball into the circle.

Science Concept

In the everyday world, everything we observe moving eventually stops.

Science Process Skill

To focus observations by using the senses.

Science Vocabulary

mark

push

roll

sign

soft, hard

stop

throw

4. Take one of the paper stop signs, walk to the ball, and place the sign on the floor at the spot where the ball stopped.

5. Now let each of the children take a turn trying to roll the ball to a stop inside the circle and then marking their spot with a paper sign. If they overshoot the mark with their first try, let them use the other ball and try to adjust their push to compensate. Have them count the number of tries they need to roll the ball into the circle.

6. Discuss with the children what they did to get their ball to stop where they wanted. You may want to use this time to discuss safety and what red stop signs mean, as when crossing streets.

Observing the Children

Do the children seem to understand the object of stopping the ball in the circle? Do they make corrections in the way the try to roll the ball to have it stop inside the circle?

ACTIVITY 6

Stop the Ball

Materials

balls in several sizes and weights

This activity allows the children to explore the physical property of momentum. By rolling the ball faster or by using a larger ball, they can change the amount of force needed to change the momentum of the balls—in this case, to stop them.

Before the Activity

Have the children bring in a ball from home if they have one.

C▪O▪N▪N▪E▪C▪T▪I▪O▪N▪S

To Language

Expressive Language - Children will vote on whether the balls will be difficult or easy to stop.

To Math

Rank Order - Children will order the balls from the most difficult to the easiest to stop.

Science Concepts

In the everyday world, everything we observe moving eventually stops.

Changing the amount or direction of an applied force results in a change in motion.

Science Process Skill

To focus observations by using the senses.

Science Vocabulary

faster, slower

harder, softer

heavier, lighter

push

stop

What to Do

1. Ask one child to stand about 5 meters (15 feet) from you. Demonstrate to the children how to roll the ball to the child. Have the child stop the ball and roll it back.

2. Now roll the ball a little harder. Ask the child if there was any difference in how hard it was to stop the ball. Have the child roll the ball back to you in a way that will make it harder for you to stop the ball. If you have a heavier ball, use it and ask the child if it is harder to stop.

3. Talk with the children about the differences in stopping the movement of the ball when it is rolled gently and when it is rolled hard. Ask: What about the heavier ball? Why was it harder to stop?

4. Use the balls the children brought from home. Hold each one up, and have the children vote on whether the ball will be easy or hard to stop. Test the ball. After all the balls have been tested, have the children rank order them from most difficult to stop to easiest to stop.

Observing the Children

Can they tell you before they actually feel the ball making contact whether it will be easy or hard to stop?

ACTIVITY 1

Log Balance Beam

Materials

large log about 2 meters in length with a 25-centimeter or larger diameter

Trees removed from construction sites, blown down in a storm, or pulled up to clear an area for building houses do not have to be wasted. By reusing them as balance beams, they can become a functional addition to your outdoor playground equipment.

Before the Activity

Arrange to have a log donated and dropped off on the playground at school. Secure the log to prevent it from rolling.

What to Do

1. Take the children outside and let them examine and freely explore the log. Encourage them to talk about the color and texture of the log. How does it compare to nearby trees?

2. After the children have had some time to explore the log, ask: Where do you think this log came from? What can we do with it? How can we use it on our playground? Responses might be, "We can walk on it, jump on it, and watch it rot."

C ∙ O ∙ N ∙ N ∙ E ∙ C ∙ T ∙ I ∙ O ∙ N ∙ S

To Language

Expressive Language - Children will talk about the color and texture of the log.

To Math

Counting - Children will count some of the rings on the log, the number of steps it takes to walk the log, and how long the log is in units of children.

Comparing - Children will hug the log and another tree to compare which is bigger.

Science Concept

Changing the amount or direction of an applied force results in a change in motion.

Science Process Skill

To focus observations by using the senses.

Science Vocabulary

balance

log

recycle

rings

tree names

trunk

3. Children will enjoy walking on the balance beam, and it will challenge their gross-motor skill development. In addition, you will be reusing a natural resource. Introduce the word *balance* as they walk on the log.

4. Have the children walk the log. Motion changes the way that the children will balance. Ask: Is it easier to balance when you are in motion or when you are still? Compare the effects of the two circumstances with the children.

5. Have the children count some of the rings on the log or count how many steps it takes to walk the log. Ask: How many children long is the log? Have the children hug the log and then another tree to compare which is bigger.

Observing the Children

Can the children discuss what the log used to be (a tree) and what it is now (a balance beam)? Are they able to relate movement (motion) with balance?

ACTIVITY 2

School-Yard Bird Survey

Materials

paper and crayons (for a Discovery Book)

clipboard

bird feeder

Showing the children your area's birds may be their introduction to an interesting hobby: bird watching. The behavior of birds is different every season. Birds mate in the spring, raise young in the summer, migrate in the fall, and find ways to survive in the winter.

Before the Activity

Place the bird feeder in the school yard a few weeks before doing this activity. The Audubon Society, one of the nation's most active environmental groups, is made up of people who like to watch birds. You may want to contact a member of this organization to help you take the children on the bird watch.

What to Do

1. Take the children on a bird-watching walk around the playground or neighborhood park. As a bird is spotted, observe what it is doing. Ask: How is it moving? Using the clipboard and paper, write the children's observations in a Discovery Book page for them to illustrate later. Try to identify and name the birds. Pigeons will move much differently from sparrows or robins.

C ▪ O ▪ N ▪ N ▪ E ▪ C ▪ T ▪ I ▪ O ▪ N ▪ S

To Language

Expressive Language - Children will describe what they see the birds doing.

Discovery Book - Children will illustrate comments about the bird walk for a class Discovery Book.

To Math

Comparing - Children will compare sizes and relative numbers of birds.

Science Concept

In the everyday world, everything we observe moving eventually stops.

Science Process Skill

To focus observations by using the senses.

Science Vocabulary

animal

bird

bird actions such as flapping and flying

bird names

2. If you don't know the name, give it a name based on its characteristics. "Black-all-over" could be the name for a grackle. The children can develop their own ways of identify birds by color, markings, or behavior, such as "the one that hangs on the side of the tree" for wood-peckers. They may also begin to pick up the bird names if you use the ones you know.

3. Ask: Are the birds the same or different? Where do we see them? Are they in water, on the ground, on a branch, on bark, in a shrub, or in a tree? Is one kind of bird more common than the others? What are the birds doing? Are they running, flapping, sleeping, sitting, eating?

4. Repeat this activity while watching at the bird feeders. Are the children aware that some birds are much more common than others?

5. Let the children illustrate the Discovery Book pages.

Observing the Children

Can the children observe the birds and use words to describe the behavior? Do they distinguish among birds and among behaviors by making comments about whether the birds or behaviors are alike or different? Do they real-ize a bird is an animal?

UNIT 3

How Objects Change

Scientists categorize change into two basic groups: physical change and chemical change. Change that merely modifies the appearance of an object is physical change. Change that actually alters the chemical makeup of an object is chemical change.

Most of the changes that young learners will come in contact with during their Discovery Science activities will be physical changes. Even if young children were to observe chemical changes, they would be very limited in their understanding of what was taking place.

Young learners should be encouraged to investigate all aspects of change. They should explore the events and objects in their immediate world that are undergoing change. How those objects change, what the new characteristics are like, and how long the process of change takes are just a few of the essential elements of change to be observed.

Science Concepts

The following science concepts will be addressed in the How Objects Change Unit:

1. Some changes are reversible; some changes are not.

2. Some change is fast; some change is slow.

3. Our senses tell us about change.

4. Some change occurs naturally; some change is caused by humans.

5. In the everyday world, some things do not appear to change.

Organizing and Presenting the Unit

Phase 1: Free Discovery

Begin Free Discovery by talking with small groups of children about how things they are familiar with go through change. Have one or more examples with you to share with the children. You might have a balloon that you can change by blowing it up. You could change a cup of water by adding one, then another color of food coloring.

Talk with the children about other changes they know about. Encourage them to think of what they might be able to do to objects to change them. As the children share their thoughts, write them on a How Objects Change Discovery Chart.

Phase 2: Conducting the Activities

The second phase of Discovery Science takes place in your classroom learning centers (described in the section on the classroom centers). Use whatever approach to center management that you have found effective. The activities in this unit are general descriptions of developmentally appropriate activities for several traditional centers. Since the children will be varied in their level of cognitive development and physical maturity, offer a wide selection of activities. Choose the activities that are appropriate for your group.

Getting Ready

Place the following materials in the Discovery Center for the children to explore during Free Discovery:

- objects that show change, such as balloons, water and food coloring, and ice cubes
- large sheet of newsprint (for a Discovery Chart)
- markers
- 5-centimeter squares of colored construction paper
- paint rollers and sleeves
- hand mirror
- clear plastic jars with lids
- 3 fishing bobbers, in different sizes
- several donut magnets
- eye droppers
- interlocking cubes
- cardboard toilet paper rolls or paper towel rolls
- flashlight
- assortment of objects that will and will not rust

Allow the children ample opportunities to investigate as many of the centers as possible, based on your time and space limitations. Some teacher assistance may be required to initiate the experience, but be careful not to over-direct the children.

Now is the time to initiate the class Discovery Books for this unit. You may want to use several books, each focused on a specific activity; a general book with drawings and captions showing what the children are learning about how objects change; or both.

As the children do the activities in the unit, encourage them to share their discoveries with you and add them to the How Objects Change Discovery Chart.

Phase 3: Making Connections to the Real World

The final phase of Discovery Science applies what the children have been experiencing in the classroom. In this phase, children make discoveries about how the concept of change is applied in the real world. These experiences will encourage the children to connect what they are learning in the classroom to adult roles and activities.

This awareness can be accomplished in several ways. You may want to invite community or family members—for example, someone who manufactures things from raw materials, a potter, or a person who knits or weaves—into the classroom to talk about their experiences with change. Another approach to making children aware of how change is a part of the world around us is to take them on a field trip. You could visit a barber shop, a hair salon, or an auto body shop. You want to children that they can observe change as an ongoing process that can be seen everywhere.

Language and Reading Center

Before you begin this unit, visit the library to select appropriate books and other resource materials to place in the Language and Reading Center. Posters and tapes will also add interest to the area, as will the display of Discovery Books, Discovery Charts, and other examples of the children's work during the unit. A number of books appropriate for this age level are listed here.

Changes by Marjorie Allen and Shelly Rotner. New York: Macmillan, 1991.

The outstanding photographs in this book illustrate the natural changes in our environment to capture the mind and eye. From the caterpillar to the butterfly, from an acorn to a giant oak, simple text engages the reader in rhythms of nature.

Spider's Web by Christine Back and Barrie Watts. Englewood Cliffs, N.J.: Silver Burdett Press, 1986.

Enjoy the photographs of flowers that make up each page as the spider's web changes.

Animals of the Night by Merry Banks. New York: Scribner Books for Young Readers, 1990.

Warm watercolor illustrations and rich language evoke the quiet nighttime life of many familiar animals that appear as children sleep.

The Very Busy Spider by Eric Carle. New York: Putnam Publishers, 1989.

Follow this smart, hardworking spider as she quietly spins her web while the other animals watch. A Carle delight!

Planting a Rainbow by Lois Ehlert. San Diego: Harcourt, Brace, Jovanovich, 1988.

Bright, colorful drawings show the reader how flowers grow from under the ground up through the soil and into gorgeous flowers.

The Seasons of Arnold's Apple Tree by Gail Gibbons. San Diego: Voyager Books/Harcourt, Brace, Jovanovich, 1988.

From watching buds grow to swinging from an apple tree's branches to enjoying its fruit, Arnold is delighted by his own secret place throughout the year.

Shadows and Reflections by Tana Hoban. New York: Greenwillow, 1990.

A collection of striking outdoor photographs depicting a variety of shadows and reflections, this book creates awareness of light sources and images in familiar surroundings.

The Snowy Day by Ezra Jack Keats. New York: Viking, 1962.

In this classic story, Peter saves a snowball in his pocket before he goes indoors. Sadly, he discovers his snowball has disappeared when he checks his pocket before bedtime.

Samuel Todd's Book of Great Inventions by E. L. Konigsburg. New York: Atheneum, 1991.

This book introduces children to the following concepts: When substances are mixed together a change occurs; colors that mix together form new colors; solids and liquids mixed together form new textures and substances.

Where Butterflies Grow by Joanne Ryder. New York: Lodestar Books, 1989.

This beautiful book follows the life cycle of a butterfly from an egg growing on the underside of a leaf to a butterfly flitting among the flowers with its companions.

Chocolate Chip Cookies by Karen Wagner. New York: Henry Holt and Co., 1990.

This delicious book guides children through the step-by-step process of making cookies. A real treat!

Owl Moon by June Yolen and John Schoenherr. New York: Philomel, 1987.

This book teaches the reader that day is light, night is dark, and objects block light to form shadows. A little girl wonders if she will ever go owling with her father. The vivid illustrations lure us into the velvety night of the forest as a brave and knowledgeable young heroine is revealed.

ACTIVITY 1

Hand-Mixing Colors

Materials

red, blue, and yellow finger-paint

spoons

finger-paint paper

paper towels (for clean up)

Finger-paint is a wonderful medium for exploring change. The children are in control as they squish, smear, and slide the finger-paint to create new colors. Let them try lots of combinations!

What to Do

1. Using two colors of paint per paper, place a spoonful of paint on opposite sides of each child's paper.

2. Tell the children to place one hand in each color. Then, have them slide their hands to the center of the paper. Encourage them to talk about what they see happening. For example, say: Where did the green come from? We only used yellow and blue. Ask: How many colors did you use?

C▪O▪N▪N▪E▪C▪T▪I▪O▪N▪S

To Language

Expressive Language - Children will use words and comparisons to describe the color changes they observe. Encourage them to talk about how the paint feels on their hands.

To Math

Counting - Children will count the colors they use.

Comparing - Children will compare the various methods they use to create new colors.

ART CENTER

Science Concept

Our senses tell us about change.

Science Process Skill

To focus observations by using the senses.

Science Vocabulary

change

color words

mix

3. When the children finish the paintings, display them.

4. Change the colors after everyone has made a painting. Using every combination of the three primary colors will create all the colors of the rainbow. Have the children compare the methods they used to create new colors.

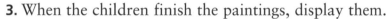

Observing the Children

Do the children realize they can mix colors to create other colors?

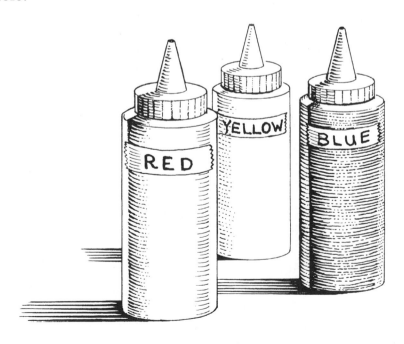

ACTIVITY 2

Ice Colors

Materials

ice cube trays

food coloring

white construction paper or other absorbent paper

paper towels (for clean up)

This is a way to mix colors using another medium: ice. Many of the children have had colored lips from eating frozen ice treats. They will quickly recognize how ice can be used as a watercolor tool. It is also interesting to see how the colors change as the paper dries.

Before the Activity

Using water colored with food coloring, fill and freeze ice cube trays. Use a variety of colors.

What to Do

1. Give each child a piece of paper. Ask: What do you think will happen if you put a piece of ice on your paper? Ask: What do you think would happen if we used these colored ice cubes? Encourage the children to share their ideas.

2. Give each child two or three colored ice cubes. Let them enjoy sliding the cubes around on the paper. Encourage them to talk about what they see.

C▪O▪N▪N▪E▪C▪T▪I▪O▪N▪S

To Language

Expressive Language - Children will describe the feel of the ice and how it changes the paper.

To Math

Comparing - Children will compare the differences between the wet and dry papers.

ART CENTER

Science Concept

Our senses tell us about change.

Science Process Skill

To focus observations by using the senses.

Science Vocabulary

change

color

dry

feel

ice

melt

mix

see (observe)

touch

wet

3. Encourage the children to talk about how the ice feels and how it changes the way the paper feels. After the cubes are melted or the children's hands get too cold, set the papers aside to dry.

4. Talk with the children about how they think their papers will change as they dry. Ask: What do you think will happen to the colors?

5. When the papers are dry, talk with the children about what they see.

Observing the Children

Can the children describe some of the differences between the wet and dry papers? Do they notice that the colors are blending?

ACTIVITY 3

Here Again, Gone Again Colors

Materials

small jar with lid

yellow corn oil

blue food coloring

water

large sheet of newsprint and markers
(for a Discovery Chart)

As the yellow oil and blue water mix, you will see green. With red water, orange will result. The children will enjoy seeing the liquids change from two colors to one and back again.

What to Do

1. Half-fill the jar with corn oil, then add water until the jar is full. Add some blue food coloring. Ask the children to tell you what they see.

2. Shake the jar to mix the oil and the blue water. Ask: What do you see now?

C ▪ O ▪ N ▪ N ▪ E ▪ C ▪ T ▪ I ▪ O ▪ N ▪ S

To Language

Expressive Language - Children will use their expressive language as they describe changes they observe as the oil and water mix and separate.

Discovery Chart - You may choose to write children's dictated responses about their observations.

To Math

Comparing - Children will compare the amounts of the two liquids. Children will compare the results that occur when the jars are shaken at different intensities.

Science Concept

Some changes are reversible; some changes are not.

Science Process Skill

To focus observations by using the senses.

Science Vocabulary

color names

harder, softer

mix

separate

shake

3. Watch with the children as the oil and water separate. Again ask: What do you see now? Talk with the children about their observations using questions such as: What do you think happened to the green? What happens when we shake the jar? What if we shake the jar harder or softer? What if we stop shaking it? Where does the green come from?

4. Encourage the children to verbalize their observations. You may want to write their responses on a Discovery Chart, or you may prefer an informal conversation.

5. Send home How Objects Change Family Connection Activity 1 (page 337).

Observing the Children

Do the children verbalize their observations of the changes from blue and yellow to green? Do they describe the changes in their own words?

ACTIVITY 4

Colors Mix Fast

Materials

several spouted cups or water bottles

water

red, blue, and yellow food coloring

plastic cups

sponges

This activity asks the children to mix colored water and then observe the changes that occur. It will probably be messy, so have sponges on hand. The children will enjoy repeating the activity. With practice, they will become quite adept at creating the secondary colors.

Before the Activity

Fill the spouted cups or water bottles with water. Add one of the colors of food coloring to each cup of water.

What to Do

1. Do this activity in an area where spilled water will not be a problem. Ask the children to mix different colors of water in the plastic cups. Have them observe the changes that take place and discuss what they see.

C▪O▪N▪N▪E▪C▪T▪I▪O▪N▪S

To Language

Expressive Language - Children will use words and comparisons to describe the changes they observe. Use this activity to reinforce the children's use of color names.

To Math

Counting - Children will count the colors used and produced.

Science Concept

Some change is fast; some change is slow.

Science Process Skill

To focus observations by using the senses.

Science Vocabulary

change

color names

fast, slow

mix

2. Let the children mix the colored waters to prepare the secondary colors green, orange, and purple. Ask: How many colors of water can you count in your cups? How many colors of water did you start with?

3. Talk with the children about the speed with which the color changes take place. Ask: Is the change fast or slow?

4. If the children have done Art Center Activity 2, Ice Colors (page 168), talk with them about their previous experiences with finger-paints. Discuss the difference between the two mixing situations—finger-paints versus colored water—and the speed with which the changes took place. When colored waters are mixed together, changed is immediate. It takes much longer to completely mix two colors of finger-paint.

Observing the Children

Do the children understand that some things mix and change more quickly than other things do?

ACTIVITY 5

Crayon Muffins

Materials

old crayons with paper removed

muffin tins

electric skillet or oven

paper

Physical change is the easiest change for the young child to observe. Crayons just change shape; their other qualities remain the same. They can be reused and perform the same function—making colored marks on paper. In addition, it is just plain fun breaking up and melting crayons.

What to Do

1. Have the children break the crayons into small pieces and put them into the muffin tins. You can have them sort crayons by color or mix colors to make rainbow crayon muffins.

2. Set the muffin tins in an electric skillet containing about 2 centimeters of water or in an oven. Caution: Do not leave crayons unattended.

3. When the crayons have melted, remove the tins and set them aside to cool. You may want to talk about how the smell of hot crayons indicates a change.

C·O·N·N·E·C·T·I·O·N·S

To Language

Expressive Language - You will talk with the children about what the crayons used to look like and how they look now. This is a good opportunity to use the words *before* and *after*.

To Math

Sorting - Children will sort crayons by color.

Science Concept

Our senses tell us about change.

Science Process Skill

To focus observations by using the senses.

Science Vocabulary

before, after

change

color names

melt

mix

shape

4. Pop the crayon muffins out of the tins. Show the children the new crayons. Ask: How did we change our crayons? How are they still the same as other crayons?

5. Let the children enjoy making pictures with the new round crayons. Talk with the children about how these crayons are different from their usual crayons.

Observing the Children

Can the children describe the changes created as they use the new crayons? Can they tell you some ways the old crayons have changed?

ACTIVITY 6

Fading Fast

Materials

squares of colored construction paper in various colors

tape

Direct sun will bleach most construction paper in a very short time. All you have to do is lay the pieces on a shelf near the window. This activity will expose children to the power of sunlight to cause change.

What to Do

1. Talk with the children about the power of the sun to do things. Make such observations as: It gives some people suntans, it warms us up, it gives us light. It does work and it can do work for us. It can also fade colors.

2. Let each child select a color square.

3. Take a sun tour of your room or building. Tell the children to find the sunniest spot they can for the sun to do its work.

C·O·N·N·E·C·T·I·O·N·S

To Language

Expressive Language - Children will use descriptive language as they talk about the color changes they observe.

To Math

Comparing - Children will compare the differences between the sunlight-exposed and non-exposed paper.

Ordering - Children may order the paper from light shades to dark shades.

Science Concept

Some change occurs naturally; some change is caused by humans.

Science Process Skill

To focus observations by using the senses.

Science Vocabulary

bleach

change

color names

comparing words, such as lighter and darker

fade

rays

sunlight

4. Let the children tape their squares in the spots they have chosen.

5. After a few days, have the children collect their squares. Talk about how the front of the paper looks and how the back of the paper looks. Ask: Did the sun change any of the colors? Did some colors change more than others? You may want to have the children order the papers from lightest to darkest shades.

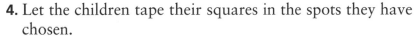

Observing the Children

Can the children tell you in their own words about the changes that occurred?

ACTIVITY 7

Paint-Roller Patterns

Materials

paint rollers

paint-roller sleeves

variety of tempera paint colors

paint-roller pans

sponges (optional)

glue (optional)

paper

sharp knife

paper towels (for clean up)

This art activity allows the children to explore patterns created by paint rollers. A smooth roller creates one design, and shapes can be cut into the roller to change the design. The children discover that the design or pattern will stay the same unless someone changes it.

Before the Activity

Prepare the paints and rollers. Use the sharp knife to cut three shapes into the rollers—a square, a triangle, and a circle. (An alternative would be to cut out the shapes from a sponge and then to glue the sponge shapes onto the rollers.) By using the standard shapes of a square, a triangle, and a circle, you can also use this activity to help the children explore shapes.

C ■ O ■ N ■ N ■ E ■ C ■ T ■ I ■ O ■ N ■ S

To Language

Expressive Language - Children will use descriptive words as they talk about the shapes and patterns they make.

To Math

Counting - Children will count the patterns they have made.

Patterning - Children will observe and talk about how the different patterns are created.

ART CENTER

Science Concept

Our senses tell us about change.

Science Process Skill

To focus observations by using the senses.

Science Vocabulary

color names

patterns

shape names

What to Do

1. Let the children use the paint and paint rollers to roll the shape patterns onto paper. After a little practice with the rollers, they will see that the same pattern is being repeated over and over.

2. Talk about the patterns that are being repeated. Notice with the children that although the colors vary from paper to paper, the patterns created by the rollers are consistent.

3. Talk with the children about the standard shapes that are part of the patterns: the square, the triangle, and the circle.

4. Ask the children: Can you count the number of patterns you have made?

Observing the Children

Do the children realize that the same pattern is repeated over and over without changing? Do they realize that though the colors may change, the pattern of each roller does not?

ACTIVITY 1

Building Additions

Materials

several different blocks sets

Polaroid camera or video camera

In this activity, you want the children to be aware of the parts of the whole that they are about to create. Their block structure goes through changes in the same way a building does as it is built. Taking pictures allows the construction to be frozen in time so comparisons can be made. Building requires slow change that we can observe.

What to Do

1. Get a small group of children excited about building something big together. Tell them you are going to take pictures of the structure as they build it. Encourage them as they work.

2. When they reach a stopping point, take a picture of what they have completed so far. Make sure they do not tear down their building.

C ▪ O ▪ N ▪ N ▪ E ▪ C ▪ T ▪ I ▪ O ▪ N ▪ S

To Language

Expressive Language - Children will use descriptive words to talk about the changes they have made in their block structure.

To Math

Comparing - Children will compare one structure to another.

Passage of Time - Children will compare pictures of structures and discuss changes made over a period of time.

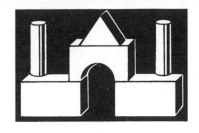

Science Concept

Some change is fast; some change is slow.

Science Process Skill

To focus observations by using the senses.

Science Vocabulary

bigger

build

change

compare

construct

higher

3. Allow as much time as you can before the children begin working on the structure again, which may be only a few minutes or overnight. When they are working again, take the opportunity to talk with them about what they have previously created and how they are changing their structure.

4. Take an new photo of the construction process. Try to capture the comparisons of what was and what is. If time allows and the builders are patient, have several periods of building, picture taking, and discussion of the changes taking place.

Observing the Children

As you share the pictures of the construction site during and after the children's building efforts, listen for comments about what has changed from what was there previously.

ACTIVITY 1

Looking Great

Materials

hand-held mirror

No matter how a child moves in front of a mirror, the image of the child remains. The image will change as the child moves, but it will never leave the mirror. Just have them try it! Every time they look, their image is looking back at them.

What to Do

1. Lead a discussion with the children about mirrors. Ask: What is a mirror? When do we use mirrors? How do mirrors help us? How do you use a mirror at home? How do you use mirrors at school? How do other people in your family use mirrors? Have you seen mirrors used in other ways?

2. Hold the mirror in front of your face. Say: If I hold this mirror and look into it, who do you think I see? Yes, I see myself. Will I always see myself when I hold the mirror in front of my face?

3. Say: Now I want you to try it. Who do you think you will see when you hold the mirror in front of your face and look into it?

4. Give the children a turn to look into the mirror and to tell who they see.

C▪O▪N▪N▪E▪C▪T▪I▪O▪N▪S

To Language

Expressive Language - Children will describe what they see in the mirror and how their image does not change.

Science Concepts

Our senses tell us about change.

In the everyday world, some things do not appear to change.

Science Process Skill

To focus observations by using the senses.

Science Vocabulary

image

look

mirror

reflect

reflection

5. Ask: Do you ever see anyone else? When? Why? Encourage the children to describe what they see in the mirror.

6. Now have the children look in the mirror with a friend and talk about how the image does or does not change.

7. The children will discover that they will constantly see the image reflected by the person or persons who are in front of and looking into the mirror. Encourage them to find ways to change their images.

Observing the Children

The children should describe how they appear every time they look into the mirror. Is there a change in the image? How does it change and how does it stay the same?

ACTIVITY 2

You Can't Lose Your Shadow

Materials

light source, such as a flashlight or desk lamp

chalk or tape

Your shadow is with you on sunny days. Is it there on cloudy days? Actually, shadows are always present—except in the dark. On sunny days they are more pronounced because blocking of the sun by the body is made more evident by the strong light.

What to Do

1. Use chalk or tape to mark a 1-meter square on the floor adjacent to a wall.

2. Have a child stand in the marked space. Shine the light on him or her. Have the children observe the child's shadow.

3. Ask the child to try to lose his or her shadow. Say: You can move any way you want, but you must stay in the square.

4. The children will discover that they can change their shapes in many ways, but it is impossible to lose their shadows. Ask: Can you make your shadows change size? Have the children compare the sizes of shadows.

C·O·N·N·E·C·T·I·O·N·S

To Language

Expressive Language - Children will use descriptive language as they talk about how their shadows move.

To Math

Comparing - Children will compare shadow sizes.

DRAMATIC PLAY CENTER

Science Concept

In the everyday world, some things do not appear to change.

Science Process Skill

To focus observations by using the senses.

Science Vocabulary

light

lose

move

shadow

Observing the Children

Do the children understand that they cannot lose their shadows?

ACTIVITY 3

Pajama Party

Materials

sleeping materials

pajamas

blankets

teddy bears and dolls

large sheet of newsprint and markers (for a Discovery Chart)

paper and crayons (for Discovery Book)

Try this fun way to review change and to use the concepts *night* and *day* to classify. Children are conscious of what they usually wear during different parts of the day. Just as night and day do not change, so what they wear and do at certain times rarely changes. Bringing night's activities into the daylight hours is a novel way to explore change with the children.

Before the Activity

Inform families ahead of time that the class will be having a pajama party. The children are to wear pajamas and bring sleeping materials, such as blankets and teddy bears.

C▪O▪N▪N▪E▪C▪T▪I▪O▪N▪S

To Language

Expressive Language - Children will describe the special things they do during the day and night. Comparisons should be expressed.

Discovery Chart - You will make one list of night things and another list of day things.

Discovery Book - Children will make drawings of what they do during the day and the night.

To Math

Comparing - The children will compare what they wear when they go to bed with what their friends wear and with what they wear during the day.

Counting - Children will talk about whether they wear more things at night or during the day.

Science Concepts

Some change occurs naturally; some change is caused by humans.

In the everyday world, some things do not appear to change.

Science Process Skill

To use observations to classify.

Science Vocabulary

change

light, dark

night, day

sky

What to Do

1. Have a special day at school designated "Pajama Party Day." On this day, the children and the teachers are to wear their pajamas and bring their blankets and favorite sleeping pals (teddy bears, dolls, blankets) to school.

2. The day should be rich in discussion about special things the children do at night such as hear a story, go to bed, and sleep. Have the children compare the ways they get ready for bed and what they wear to bed. Have them count the number of items of clothing they put on to go to bed. Ask: Do you wear more clothes during the day or during the night?

3. Try to do all the favorite night things the children suggest. Special characteristics about the night—such as the appearance of the sky, stars, moon, and darkness—can also be discussed.

4. Make a Discovery Book. Have the children make drawings of what they do during the day and the night. Caption the drawings with their comments to create a book.

5. End the day with a Discovery Chart dictated by the children. "At night time we usually. . . ." "At day time we usually. . . ."

Observing the Children

The children should be able to discuss the ways in which they change under different situations—in this case, day and night.

ACTIVITY 1

Bring It on Board

Materials

small jars with lids

plastic containers with lids

materials of different weights, such as plastic or wooden spoons, rocks, fishing weights, corks, and metal washers

water table or large, flat container filled with water

This activity allows the children to investigate what happens when objects are added to a floating jar "boat." They can compare the objects that will sink their boats to objects that can be floated by their boats.

What to Do

1. Float a closed jar on the water in front of children. Discuss what the jar is doing. Say: Let's pretend this is a boat.

2. Remove the lid, and place a large, heavy object in the bottle as you tell the children you are bringing the object *aboard* the boat. The object should not be heavy enough to sink the bottle. Discuss what happens.

3. Select a heavier object, one that will sink the bottle. Repeat the process of placing the jar in the water. Talk about what happens.

C ▪ O ▪ N ▪ N ▪ E ▪ C ▪ T ▪ I ▪ O ▪ N ▪ S

To Language

Expressive Language - Children will discuss which objects can be floated by their boats and which objects will sink. Some children maybe able to even tell you why!

To Math

Comparing - Children will compare the objects that will stay afloat to those that sink to the bottom.

Science Concept

Our senses tell us about change.

Science Process Skill

To use observations to classify.

Science Vocabulary

aboard

heavy, light

large, small

sink, float

4. Allow the children to explore with several more objects and containers. Ask: Which objects let the bottle boat float and which sink the boat? Have the children group the objects in these two categories. Discuss the size, weight, and other characteristics of the objects in the groups. Ask: Why do some objects float and some sink the boat?

Observing the Children

Do the children realize that the heavier an object is the more likely it is to sink the boat?

ACTIVITY 2

Magnet Search

Materials

3 fishing bobbers of different sizes

pieces of string

several donut magnets

water table or large, flat container filled with water

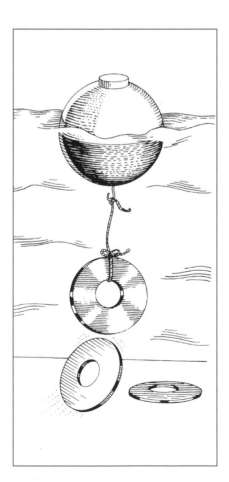

Children who have had fishing experience will be able to tell others about what happens to a bobber when they get a bite. At the water table, they will discover that a floating bobber can be made to sink by adding more and more magnetic weights. Can they think of other ways to sink a bobber?

Before the Activity

Tie one end of a string to a donut-shaped magnet. Make a loop in the other end of the string so the bobber can be hooked to the string. The string should be short enough that the magnet hangs down from the bobber a few inches from the bottom of the water table. You may have to experiment until you get the proper length. Put several magnets in water table or container.

C ▪ O ▪ N ▪ N ▪ E ▪ C ▪ T ▪ I ▪ O ▪ N ▪ S

To Language

Expressive Language - Children will use descriptive language to discuss what is taking place.

To Math

Counting - Children will count magnets as they are pulled from the bottom.

Comparing - Children will compare the number of magnets each bobber can float.

Science Concept

Our senses tell us about change.

Science Process Skill

To use observations to classify.

Science Vocabulary

attract

biggest, smallest

bobber

float, sink

lower, higher

magnet

What to Do

1. Demonstrate to the children how the bobber and magnet device can float over a magnet and pull it off the bottom of the container. Discuss with the children what is happening.

2. Select a child to use the device to pull more magnets from the bottom. Have the children count the magnets as they are picked up. Ask: What is happening to the bobber? It sinks lower and lower. Eventually it cannot pick up any more magnets from the bottom. Observe that the children have changed the bobber from something that floats to something that sinks.

3. Repeat this process with the other two bobbers. Keep the retrieved magnets in separate stacks to be discussed later.

4. Place the magnet stacks by the bobber used to pick them up. Compare the different number of magnets each bobber can float. Ask: Which bobber picks up the most magnets? Is it the biggest bobber? Does the same thing happen when you try it again?

Observing the Children

Can the children tell you which bobber can float the most magnets? Does the number change when they try it again?

ACTIVITY 1

Water into Ice, Isn't That Nice?

Materials

small cups, such as paper condiment cups from restaurants

permanent marker

tray that will fit in the freezer

toothpicks

water

potted plants

freezer

The children have probably been introduced to water freezing and forming ice. This activity is a simple review of the process, but this time we want you to focus the children's attention on change. The water changes into ice because of the cold temperature. The ice can change back to water. It is a wonderful phenomenon.

What to Do

1. Talk with the children about the activities they have done involving ice. Ask: What do you know about ice? Encourage them to share things they know in addition to their classroom experiences.

2. Ask: How can we make ice? Most children at this age will know you can put water in the freezer to make ice.

3. Using the permanent marker, make a cup for each child by putting their initials on the bottom of the cup. Have them fill their cups with water, place a toothpick in them, and set them on the freezer tray. Have the children feel the water and talk about its temperature.

4. Place the tray of cups in the freezer. Say: Tomorrow we will look at the cups to see if the ice is ready. Let the children observe the freezer to see how cold it is.

C•O•N•N•E•C•T•I•O•N•S

To Language

Expressive Language - Children will talk about the changes they feel and see.

To Math

Counting - Children will count the number of ice cubes made. They will count the number placed with each plant.

Science Concept

Some changes are reversible; some changes are not.

Science Process Skill

To focus observations by using the senses.

Science Vocabulary

cold

cool

freeze

freezer

ice

melt

temperature

warm

5. The next day, take the children to the freezer and remove the tray. Ask: How does the water look now? Can you count the number of ice cubes we made? Help the children find their own cups. Discuss how the water changed because it was very cold in the freezer. Say: Feel your ice. How is it different from the water you felt yesterday?

6. By the time the discussion is complete, the ice should be melting around the edges. Tell the children they are going to let the ice change back into water by placing the ice on the soil around the plants. As the ice cubes melt, they will supply water to the plant.

8. Using the toothpicks as handles, have the children remove the ice from the cups and lay them on the soil around the plants in the room. Have them count the number of ice cubes that go on the soil around each plant. Observe the ice periodically. The toothpicks will mark the spots where the ice changed back to water.

9. Send home How Objects Change Family Connection Activity 2 (page 337).

Observing the Children

Can the children tell you about the different states of water they observed? Can they tell you that ice is formed when water is very cold or placed in a freezer and that ice can change back to water?

ACTIVITY 2

Bubble Jars

Materials

jars and bottles with lids, in a variety of sizes and shapes

colored dish soap

water

teaspoons

The bubble jar is a way to introduce the children to the replicability of some changes. Just collect several different bottles and jars with lids, and then make bubble jars for the children to use and reuse. After a few hours, the bubbles will settle enough to be ready for the children to change them again.

What to Do

1. Show the children how to make bubble jars. Place a teaspoon of dish soap in one of the jars, fill the jar half full with water, and put on the lid.

2. Say: Look at the water and the soap in this jar. What do you see? The children should be able to see both the soap and the water.

3. Ask: How can I change this soap and water to bubbles? After you shake the jar, ask the children to describe what they see.

C▪O▪N▪N▪E▪C▪T▪I▪O▪N▪S

To Language

Expressive Language - Children will describe how the liquid changes when they shake the jars.

To Math

Comparing - Children will compare the sizes of bubbles. They will also compare the number of shakes needed to fill each jar with bubbles.

Science Concept

Some changes are reversible; some changes are not.

Science Process Skill

To focus observations by using the senses.

Science Vocabulary

alike, different

bubbles

descriptive words for the bubbles

repeat

round

4. Let the children use the variety of containers you have provided to make their own bubble jars. Encourage them to talk about how the liquid changes when they shake the jars. Ask: Where else have you seen bubbles?

5. Have the children compare the sizes of the bubbles. Ask: Are the bubbles in the jars all the same? Do the bubbles in the bigger jars look the same as the bubbles in the smaller jars?

6. Set the jars aside for awhile. Ask the children to observe the jars periodically and to comment on the changes they see. After the bubbles have settled, ask: Can you make the bubbles come back?

Observing the Children

Can the children tell you how the liquid changes when they shake the jars? Can they tell you how to make the bubbles return?

ACTIVITY 3

Seed Surprises

Materials

dishpans or water table half filled with slightly moist (not wet) soil

variety of quickly sprouting seeds, such as radishes, alfalfa, corn, and beans

fresh potting soil

scoops, spoons, or small trowels

small flowerpots

paper, seeds, and crayons (for a Discovery Book)

This activity is based on surprise. The pretend planting allows the children to use their imaginations. Then comes the surprise: all those seeds begin to sprout! This gives the children food for thought: what caused the change?

What to Do

1. At the water table or dishpans, have the children mix seeds with potting soil. Encourage the children to fill and empty the pots and to pretend to plant the seeds. Let the children play with the seeds and soil for several days. Keep the soil moist during this time of exploration.

2. After a few days, some of the seeds will begin to sprout. Show your excitement as you ask: Where did those plants come from? What happened?

3. Have the children share their ideas. Ask them to describe similarities and differences they see between the seeds and the new sprouts. Has their been a change?

C ▪ O ▪ N ▪ N ▪ E ▪ C ▪ T ▪ I ▪ O ▪ N ▪ S

To Language

Expressive Language - Children will talk about the changes they observe.

Discovery Book - Children will make drawings to show how seeds change.

To Math

One-to-One Correspondence - One-to-one correspondence will be made between the seed and the resulting germinated seed.

Science Concept

Some change is fast; some change is slow.

Science Process Skill

To focus observations by using the senses.

Science Vocabulary

grow

plant

seed

seed names

soil

sprout

4. Gently pull out some of the emerging sprouts. Pot a few and water them. Help the children observe what happens as the sprouts continue to grow.

5. Add the children's observations to a Discovery Book, and let the children illustrate them. You can record the children's comments on their drawings.

6. Let each child choose a seed to glue on a page. Have them draw how the seed changed. Put the drawings in the Discovery Book.

Observing the Children

Are the children able to describe some differences between the seeds and the sprouts? Do the children discuss change as they observe the sprouts each day?

ACTIVITY 4

Sprouts Galore!

Materials

dishpan, aquarium, or water table

assorted seeds, such as radish, zinnia, lima bean, corn, and peas

paper towels

water

Seeds produce sprouts: they change from inanimate objects into living, growing things. Sprouts from the same type of seed are the same, but sprouts look similar even if they are from different seeds. The change in some seeds is slow, but several will sprout overnight.

What to Do

1. Have the children line the bottom of the container with paper towels three or four deep. Pour in enough water to saturate the towels, but not enough to leave standing water.

2. Let the children sprinkle a variety of seeds on the paper towels. Talk with them about what the different seeds look like. Ask: Can you count the seeds?

3. Over the next several days, keep the towels moist and periodically observe the seeds with the children.

C▪O▪N▪N▪E▪C▪T▪I▪O▪N▪S

To Language

Expressive Language - Children will talk about what they see happening.

To Math

Sorting - Children may sort different types of seeds.

Counting - Children will count the seeds used.

Science Concept

Some change is fast; some change is slow.

Science Process Skill

To focus observations by using the senses.

Science Vocabulary

plant

seed

seed names

sprout

4. Talk with the children about changes they see as the seeds begin to sprout. Ask them to describe the differences they see among the sprouts. Ask: How does watering seeds change them?

5. Give the children some more seeds and have them sort the seeds (optional).

Observing the Children

Can the children use words or pictures to describe how the seeds looked before and after they were watered?

ACTIVITY 5

Keeps on Growing

Materials

grass seed

potting soil

small paper cups

small spoons

scissors

interlocking cubes or other items for measuring (optional)

The first change the children observe is the seeds sprouting and growing into grass. Then they cause a change: they cut the grass. What happens next?

What to Do

1. Ask: Do you know what grass looks like? Where have you seen it? The children may respond with "in the yard" or "in the park or on the ground." Ask the children to describe how they have seen people take care of grass at their house or at a park. Show the children the grass seed. Explain that the seed will grow into grass. Say: For this grass seed to grow, we must plant them in some soil.

2. Let the children prepare containers to plant their grass seed. Give a paper cup to each child. Have them fill their cups almost to the top with the potting soil. They can do this with their hands or with small spoons.

3. Give each child a small amount of grass seed. Demonstrate how to plant the seed.

C▪O▪N▪N▪E▪C▪T▪I▪O▪N▪S

To Language

Expressive Language - Children will describe grass and where they have seen it.

To Math

Measuring - Children may measure the height of the grass before and after cutting.

Science Concept

Some change is fast; some change is slow.

Science Process Skill

To focus observations by using the senses.

Science Vocabulary

grass

grow

lawn

plant

potting soil

sprout

4. After the seeds are planted, ask the children what they think we will need to do now. Some may know that the seeds will need water. The importance of creating a proper environment for growth can be expanded upon, but do this only after the children have contributed their thoughts. Be sure they hear that soil, water, and sunlight are the necessary ingredients.

5. Observe the containers over the next two weeks as the grass begins to grow.

6. After the grass has grown to a height of 2 to 3 centimeters, ask the children: What change would happen if we cut a bit off the top of the grass? Do you think it will grow tall again or change in some other way? Do you think it will stay the same size? Let the children make predictions.

7. You may want the children to measure the height of the grass with interlocking cubes or another unit of measurement. Then they can measure the height again after it is cut.

8. Let the children cut their grass.

9. Continue to water the grass and give it sunlight. Observe it over the next several days. Ask: What is happening? What happens to the grass that grows outside? Have you ever seen grass being cut?

Observing the Children

Can the children tell you how the seeds changed? Can they tell you how the grass changed after it was cut?

ACTIVITY 6

Lumpy, Bumpy Play Clay

Materials

Play Clay

spoons

textured material, such as coffee grounds, dry oatmeal, sand, and cornmeal

large sheet of newsprint and markers (for a Discovery Chart)

The key to this activity is for you to observe the children as they manipulate and change clay. The children's comments and answers to your questions should give you an idea of how well they understand the concepts of change and about their ability to manipulate change.

Before the Activity

Make the Play Clay.

What to Do

1. Give each child a half cup of Play Clay. Talk with them about how clay feels. Let them take a spoonful of one or more substances and mix it in with their Play Clay. Have them count the number of spoonfuls of each substance they mix with their clay.

2. Ask: What does your clay feel like now? Does it feel bumpy, crunchy, or sandy? Say: Tell me some more words to describe it. Close your eyes and talk about what you feel. You may need to continue to supply words for the children's experimentation, as at this age they are just beginning to use descriptors.

C ▪ O ▪ N ▪ N ▪ E ▪ C ▪ T ▪ I ▪ O ▪ N ▪ S

To Language

Expressive Language - Children will expand their use of descriptive language. You will provide words for them and encourage them to come up with their own words.

Discovery Chart - You will list the words the children use as the Play Clay is made and talked about.

To Math

Counting - Children will count the spoonfuls of substances they add to the Play Clay.

Science Concepts

Some change occurs naturally; some change is caused by humans.

Our senses tell us about change.

Science Process Skill

To focus observations by using the senses.

Science Vocabulary

change

half a cup

ingredients

measuring cup

mix

mixture

texture words

3. Ask the children to trade Play Clay with a friend. Say: Does your friend's clay feel the same? How does it feel the same? How does it feel different?

4. Write down the words the children use on a Discovery Chart, realizing that many of them will be using words you have supplied. When the list is complete, read it back to them. Can they think of any more texture words?

Observing the Children

Can the children tell you what they did to change their clay? Can they use some words to describe the change?

Play Clay

Ingredients	250 ml (1 cup) flour
	125 ml ($\frac{1}{2}$ cup) salt
	30 ml (2 T.) vegetable oil
	water added in small amounts to a maximum of
	125 ml ($\frac{1}{2}$ cup)

Directions No cooking is required. Mix the flour and salt and pour the oil into the mixture. Add water a little at a time until the clay has a workable consistency. Store in a plastic bag or an airtight container.

ACTIVITY 7

Light Finders

This activity allows you to introduce change through the use of many light sources. As the children react to the change, you can introduce the light sources. The children will soon expect that a new light source will appear and change the room from dark to light.

Materials

empty toilet paper or paper towel rolls

flashlight

candle

chemical light stick

lamp

gluesticks

scrap pieces of cloth

paper

crayons

large sheet of newsprint and markers (for a Discovery Chart)

Before the Activity

Select a room to darken. Set up a table or other area with the light sources you have collected.

What to Do

1. Have the children decorate the paper rolls using paper, scrap material, and crayons to create Light Finders. Tell them not to cover the ends of the rolls.

2. Ask: How do you think light helps you? The children will respond with their ideas. One or more will probably indicate that light helps them to see. You can explain that the sun is our ultimate source of light, and you can talk with them about being afraid of the dark. Without coercing participation, a spirit of adventure may encourage some children to view darkness in a friendlier way.

C ▪ O ▪ N ▪ N ▪ E ▪ C ▪ T ▪ I ▪ O ▪ N ▪ S

To Language

Expressive Language - Children will describe the sources of light they observe and how they change the appearance of the room.

Discovery Chart - Children will list as many light sources as they can.

To Math

Counting - Children will count the light sources.

Science Concepts

Some change occurs naturally; some change is caused by humans.

Our senses tell us about change.

Science Process Skill

To focus observations by using the senses.

Science Vocabulary

light sources names

light, dark

sun

3. Move into the room you have selected and darken it. Cover doors, pull shades or drapes over windows, and turn off the lights. Ask: Where does our light come from? Use your Light Finders to look around the room to see if you can find some places where there is light. (For example, they may see light coming in around the door.) When you see something that is giving light, tell me so I can look at it, too. Some of the children may spot light coming in a window. Ask: Where do you think that light is coming from?

4. Turn on the flashlight. Say: Yes, light is coming from this flashlight. It helps us see better in the room. Repeat this process as you light the lamp, the candle, and the room lights. The children will focus on the light source each time. Have the children count the number of different light sources they have seen. Encourage them to talk about how light changes the way the room looks.

5. Discuss the various light sources that the children see on the way to and from school, such as traffic lights, headlights, and street lights. Make a Discovery Chart as children share their knowledge of the many light sources they know.

Observing the Children

Can the children tell you how light changes the room? Can they indicate sources of light in the room?

ACTIVITY 8

Gravity Tester

Materials

cardboard box with a sliding, removable base (reinforce with tape to make it sturdy)

objects to place in the box, such as a ball, block, button, spool, and toy car

Somewhere in the children's scientific training they will deal with the constancy of gravity. At this age, all they can understand is that anything that is dropped always falls. It is something that never changes.

Before the Activity

Make the gravity tester, a box with a removable base.

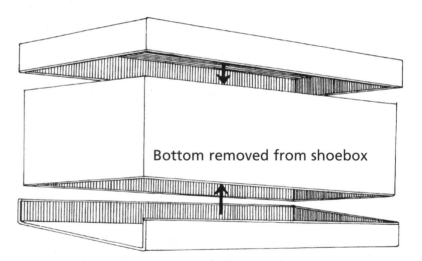

Bottom removed from shoebox

End removed from second shoebox top

C▪O▪N▪N▪E▪C▪T▪I▪O▪N▪S

To Language

Expressive Language - Children will be introduced to the word gravity as they relate to what happens.

To Math

Counting - Children will count the objects that drop.

Science Concept

In the everyday world, some things do not appear to change.

Science Process Skill

To focus observations by using the senses.

Science Vocabulary

change

drop

fall

gravity

predict

unchangeable

What to Do

1. Talk with the children about gravity. Explain that it is a force that pulls objects to the ground. (Note: In your discussion about gravity causing anything that drops to fall, one of the children may ask about helium balloons staying aloft. Answer the question with an experiment. Purchase an inexpensive *rubber* balloon filled with helium. Observe it for several days, until it settles to the floor. If the question of birds and flight arises, ask the children if they have ever seen a bird light on a limb or on the ground. Go outside to watch for bird to land.)

2. Let the children place objects in the gravity tester. Ask them to predict which objects will fall to the floor when the bottom is removed from the box. (This is accomplished by pulling on the cardboard base so it slides out from under the box.)

3. Repeat the procedure with other items the children choose to place in the box. Have the children count the objects that drop.

4. The children will observe that regardless of what object they place in the box, it will always fall to the floor when the base is removed.

Observing the Children

After experimenting with the gravity tester, the children should be able to tell you what will always happen when they use the gravity tester.

ACTIVITY 9

Mixing Things with Water

Materials

clear plastic cups or small jars

spoons

labeled container of salt

labeled container of white sand

labeled container of sugar

water

Most young children enjoy mixing things in water. The procedure yields consistent results: it can be repeated again and again without a change: salt always dissolves, sand never does.

C·O·N·N·E·C·T·I·O·N·S

To Language

Expressive Language - Children will describe what they see happening. They will be introduced to the scientific term *dissolve*.

To Math

One-to-One Correspondence - The children will use one spoonful of salt or sand for one cup of water.

Science Concept

Our senses tell us about change.

Science Process Skill

To focus observations by using the senses.

Science Vocabulary

dissolve

mix

mixture

salt

What to Do

1. Give each child two cups of water and a spoon. Tell the children to put a spoonful of salt in one cup and a spoonful of sand in the other cup. Ask: What do you see?

2. Now have them stir the water. Ask: What changes do you see?

3. Talk with the children about the change that occurred: the salt *dissolved* in the water and the sand did not.

4. Have the children repeat the dissolving activity with sugar in another cup. Ask them to compare what happens with the sugar in water to what happens with the salt and the sand in water.

Observing the Children

Can the children describe the differing outcomes?

ACTIVITY 10

Is It Really Gone?

Materials

3 clear plastic cups

spoons

salt

sugar

sand

eye droppers

black paper

water

This activity asks the children to look at the results of their dissolving salt and sugar in water. Their talking and guessing about what will happen as the water evaporates can provide experiences that will lead to a partial understanding of physical reactions. The substances that are left behind can be dissolved, and the evaporation process can be repeated. This never-ending cycle is repeated daily on our planet.

Before the Activity

Mix a spoonful of salt in a cup of water, a spoonful of sugar in a second cup, and spoonful of sand in a third cup. Label the cups with the words *salt, sugar,* and *sand,* or, if the children have completed Discovery Center Activity 9, Mixing Things with Water (page 208), let them use their own cups for this activity. You may also choose to have them make new solutions for this activity.

C · O · N · N · E · C · T · I · O · N · S

To Language

Expressive Language - Children will describe what they see happening. They can use the scientific term *dissolve* to describe what they see.

To Math

Counting - Children will count the number of drops of liquid they put on the paper.

DISCOVERY CENTER

Science Concept

Our senses tell us about change.

Science Process Skill

To focus observations by using the senses.

Science Vocabulary

dissolve

evaporate

mixture

solution

What to Do

1. If the children have completed Mixing Things with Water (page 208), review with them what happened when they mixed sugar, sand, or salt with water.

2. Encourage the children to compare the appearances of the sugar water, salt water, and sand water. Ask them how the mixtures are the same and how they are different.

3. Ask the children what they think will happen if they let the water in the solutions dry out of the mixtures.

4. Have each child use a dropper to put a few drops of water from each container onto a piece of black paper. Have them count the drops of water as they fall.

5. Have the children let the water on the papers evaporate. Explain what *evaporate* means: the water is going into the air and leaving what was *in* the water behind (on the paper).

6. Talk with the children about what they see after the water evaporates.

Observing the Children

How do the children describe the differences between the sugar, sand, and salt? Can they tell you that a white residue was left for the salt and sugar and not for the sand?

ACTIVITY 1

Star Chamber

Materials

large box, such as a refrigerator packing box, for the children to stand in

luminescent stick-on stars

black construction paper (optional)

masking or duct tape to cover box seams

flashlight

paper (optionally cut into large stars) and crayons (for a Discovery Book)

The star chamber, your own classroom planetarium, provides excitement and a new way of exploring change and darkness. To see how a small light changes darkness is a revelation for the child. The glow-in-the-dark stars provide another element of change to experience in your new classroom planetarium.

What to Do

1. Prepare the star chamber with assistance from the children. This is a critical step, as some young children have a fear of darkness. The children can paint and decorate the outside of the box with creations that depict the night sky. Cover the interior of the box with black construction paper (optional), then decorate the interior with the luminescent stick-on stars.

2. Have two children go into the star chamber with the flashlight. When they enter, the light will cause the stars to glow for a while. Have the children observe the stars. Tell them not to use the flashlight until they find out how well they can see without any light.

3. Now have the children turn on the flashlight. They will discover that they can see. Light is always required to see. They will see the stick-on stars as well. Ask: What

C ▪ O ▪ N ▪ N ▪ E ▪ C ▪ T ▪ I ▪ O ▪ N ▪ S

To Language

Expressive Language - Children will talk about what they see inside the star chamber.

Discovery Book - Children will draw what they saw in the star chamber and dictate their comments.

Science Concept

In the everyday world, some things do not appear to change.

Science Process Skill

To focus observations by using the senses.

Science Vocabulary

dark

glow

light

night

planetarium

sky

star

happens to the stars when you turn off the flashlight? Have the children talk about what they see inside the star chamber. Talk about real stars and other things they see at night.

4. Let other child have turns in the star chamber.

5. Have each child create a star page for a Discovery Book. They may draw what they saw in the star chamber and dictate comments. You may also have them use star-shaped paper to make a "star" Discovery Book.

Observing the Children

Do the children understand the need for light in order to see?

ACTIVITY 2

Leaves Change

Materials

leaves

string or long strip of paper

tape or clothespins

Individualize the children's experiences with change by having each child select a leaf to observe. The children will notice that some leaves they have collected change more quickly than others. Do they also notice different types of change?

What to Do

1. Go for a leaf walk. Let the children feel different leaves. Caution: Make sure the children stay clear of poison oak, poison ivy, and sumac. Explore and talk about the variations in texture, color, size, and shape among the different leaves.

2. Before returning from the walk, have each child pick one leaf to take back to the classroom.

3. Have the children show their leaves and then count the numbers of the same kinds of leaves that they have chosen.

C ▪ O ▪ N ▪ N ▪ E ▪ C ▪ T ▪ I ▪ O ▪ N ▪ S

To Language

Expressive Language - Children will describe the different leaves and variations such as texture, color, size, and shape.

To Math

Counting - Children will count the number of the same kind of leaf.

Time Passing - Children will observe how leaves change over time.

Science Concept

Some change is fast; some change is slow.

Science Process Skill

To focus observations by using the senses.

Science Vocabulary

change

color words

leaf names

texture words

wilt

4. Hang the leaves in the room by taping or pinning them to a string clothesline or to a large piece of paper.

5. Throughout the day, call the children's attentions to the leaves. Talk about the changes they notice. Some leaves will change more than others. Talk about how the leaves change over time. For example, compare how the leaves look in the morning to how they look in the afternoon.

6. With the children, continue to observe the leaves for a few days or until further changes are no longer apparent. Help the children think of words that describe the changes as the leaves wilt.

Observing the Children

Do the children identify the changes that occur? Do they realize that not all leaves change in the same way?

ACTIVITY 3

Short Legs, Long Legs

Materials

several objects of various heights and lengths, such as pieces of yarn and blocks

The human body has a tall, slender shape. Our long legs are very useful for running, stepping, and especially walking. We do not appreciate how well these long legs of our work until they become short. In this activity, children try a "short" walk.

What to Do

1. Talk with the children about why they think we have long legs and what we can do with our long legs. Ask them what they think it would be like if their legs were suddenly shorter.

2. Have the children get down on their knees. Ask: What has happened to us now? Will this will change what we can do?

3. Lay the pieces of yarn on the floor. Have the children to try to step over the outstretched yarn without touching it. Lay out several blocks in a row and see if they can step over the blocks while on their knees.

C▪O▪N▪N▪E▪C▪T▪I▪O▪N▪S

To Language

Expressive Language - Children will talk about how their bodies move differently in the two positions.

Science Concept

Our senses tell us about change.

Science Process Skill

To focus observations by using the senses.

Science Vocabulary

knees

short, long

4. Have the children try various tasks, both on their knees and standing up. Discuss with them which was easier. Ask: What could you and couldn't you do with your "short legs"?

Observing the Children

Ask the children to tell you if they need to be on their long legs or short legs to do specific tasks.

Snowball Melting

ACTIVITY 4

Materials

snow or crushed ice

large container

plates

paper towels

large sheet of newsprint and markers
(for a Discovery Chart)

Children know that snow and ice melt. You can relate this activity to Discovery Center Activity 1, Water into Ice, Isn't That Nice? (page 192) as you show how the ball of snow changes into water as it melts. Putting the snowballs in order by size is one way of indicating how fast each will melt.

What to Do

1. Talk about what happens to snowballs when they are left in a hot place. Talk with the children about their experiences with snow. Ask them where they have seen snow melt.

C ▪ O ▪ N ▪ N ▪ E ▪ C ▪ T ▪ I ▪ O ▪ N ▪ S

To Language

Expressive Language - Children will describe what happens as the snowballs melt.

Discovery Chart - You will record the children's estimations.

To Math

Ordering - Children will place the snowballs in order from largest to smallest.

Estimating - Children will predict what the melting order will be.

Science Concepts

Some change is fast; some change is slow.

Some changes are reversible; some changes are not.

Science Process Skill

To use observations to classify.

Science Vocabulary

change

cold

estimate

heat

melt

temperature

2. Use the container filled with crushed ice or snow. Have each child make a snowball and put it on a plate. When they are done, help them order the snowballs by size from largest to smallest.

3. Ask the children to indicate which snowball will melt first and which will melt last. Write their thoughts on a Discovery Chart. Talk about what they think will happen.

4. Observe the snowballs as they melt to see if the predictions were accurate. Ask the children to talk about the changes they see.

Observing the Children

Can the children talk about what happened as the snowballs melted?

ACTIVITY 5

Make Them Rust

Materials

white paper towels

dishpan or other container

salt

objects that will rust, such as nails, washers, and springs

objects that will not rust, such as plastic buttons and plastic paper clips

Objects can be seen rusting throughout the world. Most objects that rust were created by humans. When an object rusts, it is being acted upon by oxygen. Wetting an iron surface and adding salt speeds up the rust process. Through this activity, the children will find that some objects—objects not made of iron—do not rust. The change in the objects allows us to sort them into two groups.

What to Do

1. Place several layers of paper towels in the dishpan. Have the children scatter the variety of objects on the paper towels.

2. Add enough water to saturate the paper towels. Sprinkle the objects with salt to accelerate the rusting process. Keep the towels wet over the next several days.

C ▪ O ▪ N ▪ N ▪ E ▪ C ▪ T ▪ I ▪ O ▪ N ▪ S

To Language

Expressive Language - Children will talk about what they see happening.

To Math

Counting - Children will count the objects that rusted.

Sort and Classify - Children will group the objects into two categories.

Tally Sheet - The number of rusty items found on the walk will be recorded.

Science Concepts

Our senses tell us about change.

Some change is fast; some change is slow.

Science Process Skill

To use observations to classify.

Science Vocabulary

iron

metal

names of rusting and nonrusting objects

rust

3. When the rust appears, have the children describe what they see happening. Have them note the rust stains surrounding some of the objects.

4. Have the children divide the objects according to those that rusted and those that did not. Ask: Can you count the things that rusted?

5. Take the children on a rust walk. How many rusty things can they find?

Observing the Children

The children should understand that some things rust and others do not. Can they divide the objects into the two groups by the objects' tendency to rust?

ACTIVITY 1

Garbage Garden

Materials

garden trowels or small shovels

tongue depressors

watering can

items to bury: pieces of wool, plastic, toilet paper, cardboard, newspaper, apple, aluminum foil, wood, and banana peel

Children enjoy digging holes. When they dig them, they are able to experience what is hidden below the surface of the earth. In this activity, children observe firsthand what soil is like and what changes take place to materials buried beneath the ground.

What to Do

1. Have the children dig holes 12 to 15 centimeters deep, one hole for each item to be buried in the garbage garden. Encourage the children to use descriptive language such as color and texture words as they talk about the items they have chosen to bury.

2. Have the children place an item in each hole, add some water, and fill in the hole with soil.

C ▪ O ▪ N ▪ N ▪ E ▪ C ▪ T ▪ I ▪ O ▪ N ▪ S

To Language

Expressive Language - Children will use color and texture words to describe the objects before they are buried and after they are dug out.

Written Language - Children will, at their own levels, create labels for the buried items.

To Math

One-to-One Correspondence - Children will need to dig one hole for each item.

Science Concept

Some change is fast; some change is slow.

Science Process Skill

To focus observations by using the senses.

Science Vocabulary

change

decay

decompose

garbage

recycle

rot

3. Place a tongue depressor where each item is buried. Let the children use symbolic writing or pictures to label the tongue depressor for each buried item. They might also dictate a label.

4. Water the garden each day for four weeks, then dig up the buried items.

5. Talk with the children about how the items look. Ask: Are they different? Have they changed? Which are just the same as when we buried them? Talk about how things decompose and help to create more soil.

Observing the Children

Children should be able to describe the changes in the objects between the time they were planted and the time they were dug up.

ACTIVITY 2

Plants Need Sun

Materials

fast-growing grass seed

trowel or sturdy spoon

rake

shovel

straw

water source

toothpicks or tongue depressors

tall stakes

strips of cloth (as flags for the stakes)

string

Choosing several sites on the school yard where plants can grow and survive the ravages of the children's running can provide excellent observational experiences. Blocking off areas might help. Plant one plot in the sun and another in the shade. Water well, cover with straw, and watch the grass grow.

What to Do

1. Have the children plant some grass seed in a sunny location in the middle of the well-worn playground. Use stakes and a length of string to keep little feet off the growth plot. Be sure the stakes are tall enough to be seen easily, and tie strips of cloth to them to make them even more visible.

2. Select a second location in a totally shaded area of the playground to plant another plot of grass.

3. Water the plots as necessary, and cover the grass seed with straw to retain moisture and enhance growth.

C▪O▪N▪N▪E▪C▪T▪I▪O▪N▪S

To Language

Expressive Language - Children will describe the change that occurs between the plants grown in the sun and the plants grown in the shade.

To Math

Measuring - Children will compare the height of the plants.

Science Concept

Some change occurs naturally; some change is caused by humans.

Science Process Skill

To focus observations by using the senses.

Science Vocabulary

change

grass

grow

plant

seeds

shade

soil

sun

4. Take the children to the plots daily so they can observe the growth of the grass. Go at different times of the day.

5. Talk about and compare the growth of grass in the two plots. Ask: What changes do you see? Is there a difference between the grass grown in the sunny plot and that grown in the shade? Give the children toothpicks or tongue depressors to compare the height of the plants in the two plots.

Observing the Children

Can the children identify the plot where grass grew the best? Do they understand that grass needs sunlight to grow?

ACTIVITY 3

Compost Bin

Materials

leaves, grass clippings, and other yard wastes

shovel or spading fork

large sheet of newsprint and markers (for a Discovery Chart)

Many people are turning to composting as a way of handling the huge amounts of yard waste that can no longer be placed in landfills. Your children can be a part of this movement by creating their own composting area. They will be able to observe the changes that take place during the composting process.

Before the Activity

Select an approved site for your compost pile.

What to Do

1. Take a trip around the school yard. Talk about the best site for a compost pile.

2. Let the children assist in making a compost pile by collecting leaves and grass clippings and carrying them to the compost site. Begin making the compost pile by laying down a layer of leaves several inches thick. Place a layer of grass on top of the leaves. Repeat this process until you have a layered pile several feet high.

C·O·N·N·E·C·T·I·O·N·S

To Language

Expressive Language - Children will use descriptive language as they talk about the composting process.

Discovery Chart - You will list the steps involved in each part of the composting process.

To Math

Time - You will talk about time passing as you and the children wait for decomposition to occur.

Science Concept

Some change occurs naturally; some change is caused by humans.

Science Process Skill

To focus observations by using the senses.

Science Vocabulary

change

compost

decay

decompose

names of animals found in the compost pile

names of items put in the compost pile

soil

3. Begin a Discovery Chart. Have the children describes the steps in the process of creating the compost pile. Add to the chart when you turn the pile and when composting is complete, letting the children describe the steps in each process.

4. Water the compost pile until it becomes uniformly moist but not soggy. You may find it necessary to water the pile again if there is little or no rainfall.

5. After several days, if your compost is working, the pile should feel warm inside—hot if things are really working. The children can feel the heat by pushing their hands into the center of the pile. Talk about time passing as you wait for the decomposition to occur.

6. Two weeks after the process has started, it is time to turn the pile. A shovel or spading fork will work fine. Show the children how to stir the compost and help them do it. Turn the pile once more in another few weeks.

7. When the pile is no longer giving off heat, the compost is ready to mix with the soil in a garden.

Observing the Children

Can the children talk about what materials were placed in the compost pile and how they changed.

UNIT 4

How Objects Are Made and Used

The activities in How Objects Are Made and Used allow you to expose the children to fundamental applications of technology. The children will begin to explore technology and to unravel answers for such important questions as, "What can we do with this? Why is this shaped the way it is?"

In this unit, the children will also have the opportunity to devise special tools for specific tasks. Imagine how a child feels when he or she invents the perfect gadget for accomplishing a feat or for helping in the classroom.

Organizing and Presenting the Unit

Phase 1: Free Discovery

Begin Free Discovery by discussing with the children what they know about tools. Have some tools available to share with them.

Ask: "Do you have any tools at home? What have you used tools for at home? Do you know anyone who uses tools? What do they do with them?" As the children share their thoughts, write them on a How Objects Are Made and Used Discovery Chart.

Phase 2: Conducting the Activities

The second phase of Discovery Science takes place in your classroom learning centers (described in the section on the classroom centers). Use whatever approach to center management that you have found effective. The activities in this unit are general descriptions of developmentally appropriate activities for several traditional centers. Since the children will be varied in their level of cognitive development and physical maturity, offer a wide selection of activities. Choose the activities that are appropriate for your group.

Allow the children ample opportunities to investigate as many of the centers as possible, based on your time and space limitations. Some teacher assistance may be required to initiate the experience, but be careful not to over-direct the children.

Science Concepts

The following science concepts will be addressed in the How Objects Are Made and Used Unit:

1. Tools are made the way they are for specific purposes.

2. We can manufacture objects to allow us to accomplish certain tasks.

Getting Ready

Place the following materials in the Discovery Center for the children to explore during Free Discovery:

- tools, such as a hammer, egg beater, and tweezers
- large sheet of newsprint (for a Discovery Chart)
- markers

Now is the time to initiate the class Discovery Books for this unit. You may want to use several books, each focused on a specific activity; a general book with drawings and captions showing what the children are learning about how objects are made and used; or both.

As the children continue to discover new tools and uses for them, encourage them to share their discoveries with you and add them to the How Objects Are Made and Used Discovery Chart. You might have the children cut out pictures of tools to add to the chart, or you may want to eventually compile a list of tools and their uses.

Phase 3: Making Connections to the Real World

The final phase of Free Discovery incorporates what the children have been experiencing in the classroom. In this phase, children make discoveries about how tools are actually used in the real world. These experiences in the application of technology will encourage the children to connect what they are learning in the classroom to adult roles and activities.

You may want to invite family members or other community helpers to show the tools they use and to talk about how they use them. Consider taking a field trip to a farm, a construction site, a small manufacturing company, or a hardware store. Consult with the children's families for other possibilities.

Language and Reading Center

Before you begin this unit, visit the library to select appropriate books and other resource materials to place in the Language and Reading Center. Posters and tapes will also add interest to the area, as will the display of Discovery Books, Discovery Charts, and other examples of the children's work during the unit. A number of books appropriate for this age level are listed here.

Machines at Work by Byron Barton. New York: Crowell, 1987.

Simple illustrations and text show construction workers on a building site using various tools during a working day.

Sanitation Workers A to Z by Jean Johnson. New York: Walker, 1988.

This alphabet book presents the sanitation worker's tools, equipment, and diverse tasks with an emphasis on the importance of this career to the community.

Fire Fighters by Robert Maass. New York: Scholastic, 1989.

The text is a little wordy for preschoolers, but the photographs are wonderful and clearly illustrate real fire fighters and all the tools they use in their jobs.

Bridges by Ken Robbins. New York: Dial, 1991.

Hand-tinted photographs and clear, brief text describe the design and structure of a variety of vehicular and pedestrian bridges. This is a fine picture book with locations of each bridge listed.

Handy Hank Will Fix It by Anne Rockwell. New York: Holt, 1988.

Hank spends a busy day fixing a plugged drain, replacing a washer, and hanging a door. Detailed text is complimented by bright illustrations in a comfortable look at small-scale technology.

The Lazy Bear by Brian Wildsmith, Brian. New York: Franklin Watts, 1974.

This book shows children how machines help make work easier and that many household items are machines. A bear climbs a wagon, then zooms down a hill. Scared but thrilled, he does it again. However, his fun is a little more like work when he has to push the wagon up the hill to go on another ride.

Everyday Things and How They Work by Mary-Jane Wilkins. New York: Warwick Press, 1991.

Take a new look at ordinary tools, appliances, and gadgets while learning about their functions. Readers are encouraged to think of new ways to use old tools.

A Visit to the Dairy Farm by Sandra Ziegler. Chicago: Childrens Press, 1987.

Follow a school class on a field trip to a dairy farm through these excellent photographs. If a child cannot visit a dairy farm, this is the next best thing.

ACTIVITY 1

Litter Printing

Materials

washable stamp pads

paper

paper bags

objects found on a walk

paper towels (for clean up)

The scavenger hunt is a wonderful way to collect objects. But do your children know that the things they find on a walk can also be used to create art? This activity calls for the children to be creative. Do it after they have had some experience with stamp pads and printers in the classroom, leaving the materials out for them to try new materials to print.

What to Do

1. Take a junk-collecting walk with the children. Have them look for anything that they might be able to use for printing. They might find things such as bottle caps, nails, screws, cans, and plastic bottles. **Caution:** Tell the children to avoid glass. During the walk, talk about what the children find and what kind of print they expect from each item.

C▪O▪N▪N▪E▪C▪T▪I▪O▪N▪S

To Language

Expressive Language - Children will describe what they find and the patterns the objects make.

Discovery Book - Children's artwork will be displayed in a class Discovery Book.

To Math

Patterning - Children may want to create patterns with their stamping objects.

ART CENTER

Science Concept

We can manufacture objects to allow us to accomplish certain tasks.

Science Process Skill

To focus observations by using the senses.

Science Vocabulary

collect

print

recycle

same

shape

2. Back in the classroom, say: Let's see what we can print from the junk we collected on our walk. Have the children press their found objects on stamp pads and then onto paper to make prints of the objects.

3. Some of the children may want to use their new stamping objects to create patterns on their paper.

4. Talk about and compare the various shapes the children have made. Ask: Does an object make the same design every time? Do some objects make similar prints?

5. Challenge the children to make more than one shape with the same object. For example, a bottle cap may be pressed flat to make a circle or rolled on its side to make a line.

6. Caption the artwork with the children's comments, and collect the pages into a Discovery Book.

Observing the Children

Do the children realize that the shape of a print is determined by the shape of the object?

ACTIVITY 2

Glue Tools

Materials

collection of items to be recycled, such as egg cartons, wood scraps, foam packing peanuts, paper cups, and straws

white glue

tape

pieces of cardboard for bases

small containers for glue

craft sticks

eye droppers

paintbrushes

Tools have value only when they are useful for performing a specific task. A big screwdriver is not useful for a tiny screw. In this activity, the children are given three tools with which to glue objects onto cardboard. Which works best for a particular job is the focus of the activity. Maybe they have to make a new tool, or maybe they will use another: their fingers. Be careful or this activity will become sticky!

Before the Activity

Have the children bring in a collection of throw-away items from home, such as paper egg cartons.

What to Do

1. Place the pieces of cardboard in the Art Center. Have one of the children select an item. Talk about what material the item is made of. Talk about the three R's: reduce, reuse, and recycle. Say: We are going to reuse some things we have collected by gluing them together on a cardboard base. We have three tools we can use to spread the glue: a dropper, a stick, and a paintbrush. You can decide what tool works best for you.

C ▪ O ▪ N ▪ N ▪ E ▪ C ▪ T ▪ I ▪ O ▪ N ▪ S

To Language

Expressive Language - Children will use relative terms such as *better* and *best*.

Science Concept

Tools are made the way they are for specific purposes.

Science Process Skill

To focus observations by using the senses.

Science Vocabulary

better, best

recycle

reduce

reuse

tool

2. Allow the children to work independently to create their own sculptures.

3. Talk with the children about how the different tools work. They might say things such as, "The glue plugged up the dropper, but the paintbrush really worked." Children this age are just beginning to understand what relative terms like *better* and *best* mean, especially objectively. For them the "best" one is often the one another child they admire chooses. That is all right. It is a start.

Observing the Children

When you talk with a child, can he or she tell you which tool worked best?

ACTIVITY 3

Little Home Builders

Materials

cardboard tubes

small boxes

egg cartons

cups

paper

string

yarn

tape

glue

scissors

A pretend home for a favorite animal or doll provides an ideal outlet for creative building. A little house, however, is easier to build than a big one, so keep the pretending small. The children can use the tools and materials at the Art Center, and items from your pile of plastic foam, cardboard, plates, and paper cups, to create homes for their toys. While the children are building their homes, you can reinforce the concept of *reuse*.

Before the Activity

Ask them to bring something to school—a doll, a robot, a stuffed animal, or the like—that they would like to build a home for.

What to Do

1. Ask the children to build a home for the item they brought from home.

C·O·N·N·E·C·T·I·O·N·S

To Language

Expressive Language - Children will describe how they build their houses.

To Math

Measurement - Children will use simple measuring skills as they compare the sizes of their toys to the houses they are making.

Science Concepts

Tools are made the way they are for specific purposes.

We can manufacture objects to allow us to accomplish certain tasks.

Science Process Skill

To focus observations by using the senses.

Science Vocabulary

construct

home

house

tool

2. Let the children, working alone or with a partner, select their own materials from the collection you have provided. Helping to design the project and building it together encourages cooperation and may be a successful approach with some of the older preschoolers.

3. As they build, they will be experimenting with balance, stability, form, and function. Ask questions, such as: Can you find a box big enough for your bear? What do you think she would like in her house? How can you find a bed that is the right size?

4. Talk with the children about what they would do without certain building tools such as tape and scissors.

Observing the Children

Can the children talk about what they used to build their houses? If the children worked with partners, talk about how they made the home suitable for both toys.

ACTIVITY 4

Build a Tree

Materials

mop or broom handle

stand for the handle (a Christmas tree stand works well)

hammer

nails

cardboard tubes

paper

string

yarn

tape

glue

paper and crayons (for a Discovery Book)

The tree is a wonderful structure. It responds to gravity and the environment to stand strong and upright. Is making a tree easy? Let's find out!

Before the Activity

Set the mop or broom handle in the stand to stay upright. Hammer several nails along the length of the handle.

What to Do

1. Ask the children to describe a tree. How does a tree grow? Take a walk out in the school yard to view a tree. Point out the branches and limbs.

2. Show the children the materials from the collection you have provided. Work with them to make the tree. As they build, they will be experimenting with balance, stability, form, and function. Problems will develop as they try to make the branches stay on the main broom handle trunk. They may have to use more tape.

C·O·N·N·E·C·T·I·O·N·S

To Language

Discovery Book - Children will draw pictures and dictate responses to "If I had a magic tree, _____ would grow on it."

Science Concept

We can manufacture objects to allow us to accomplish certain tasks.

Science Process Skill

To focus observations by using the senses.

Science Vocabulary

branches

build

leaves

limbs

pretend

real

tool

tree

trunk

3. Talk with the children about what they would do without a building tool such as tape. Would the absence of the nails make a difference? **Caution:** Remind the children to be careful so they don't scratch themselves on the nails.

4. Discuss how their tree is like and different from a real tree. Talk about *real* and *pretend*.

5. Write a book titled *The Magic Tree*. Have the children draw pictures and dictate responses to "If I had a magic tree, _____ would grow on it."

Observing the Children

Can the children talk about what they used to build their tree? What tools made the job easy? What was difficult to do?

If I had a magic tree, POPCORN would grow on it.

ACTIVITY 5

Balancing Crayons

Materials

crayons

double-pan balance

The balance is a tool we can use to find which is the heavier of two objects or how much something weighs. Which set of crayons has the greatest mass? The balance will help us find out.

What to Do

1. Have the children select two colors of crayons to compare using the balance. For example, ask: Which do you think there are more of, red crayons or blue crayons?

2. Have them sort the red and blue crayons, putting one color on each side of the balance. The level of the balance will change as they place more crayons in the pans. Watch as this happens. Say: Now the red side is going down. The reds are heavier. What happens when we put some more crayons on the blue side?

C▪O▪N▪N▪E▪C▪T▪I▪O▪N▪S

To Language

Expressive Language - Children will use comparative language.

To Math

Sorting - Children will sort crayons by color, initially just looking for two colors. With experience, they will be able to make piles of several different colors at the same time.

Weighing and Comparing - Children will begin to understand that a balance is a tool to help them compare mass.

ART CENTER

Science Concept

Tools are made the way they are for specific purposes.

Science Process Skill

To focus observations by using the senses.

Science Vocabulary

balance

color names

compare

heavy, heavier, heaviest

level

light, lighter, lightest

weigh

3. When no more red or blue crayons can be found, have the children determine which side is heavier.

4. Three- and four-year-old children are beginning to use comparative language. You will often hear them say, "I'm the biggest," whether they are or not. As you work with this activity, verbalize your observations of their actions. Say, for instance: You made that side go up. The reds are the heaviest. I wonder which will be lighter?

5. Encourage the children to repeat the activity with other colors. Some children may be able to find which color set is the heaviest of all.

Observing the Children

Can the children identify which side of the balance contains the greatest mass?

ACTIVITY 6

Water Inventions

Materials

variety of containers that will hold water, such as a glasses, pottery bowls, plastic jugs, foil pans, paper cups, and small boxes

materials for constructing containers that will hold water, such as oil-based clay, foil, waxed paper, tape, stapler, and glue

water

paper towels (for clean up)

You never know when you will be lost in the jungle or out in the desert and have to make a container to hold water. It will never happen? OK, but it is fun for the children to pretend as they explore materials to create a container to hold water.

What to Do

1. Pour water back and forth among the various containers. Talk with the children about how many things can hold water. Ask them to think of some other things that hold water.

2. Say: Today you are going to make your own container to hold water. You can make any kind of container you want to make out of anything you want to use. When your container is finished, we will pour in some water and see if it works.

C▪O▪N▪N▪E▪C▪T▪I▪O▪N▪S

To Language

Expressive Language - Children will describe their containers and how they worked.

To Math

Comparing and Predicting - Children will predict which of two containers will hold more water.

Science Concept

We can manufacture objects to allow us to accomplish certain tasks.

Science Process Skill

To focus observations by using the senses.

Science Vocabulary

container

fix

leak

material

pour

repair

test

3. Encourage and support the children as they work on their containers. If a container leaks when tested, ask questions that might help the children think of ways to fix it. Give them enough time to try and try again.

4. Once all the containers have been filled, tested, repaired, and retested, choose one of the child-constructed containers. Have the children predict which container will hold more, yours or the child's. Test the predictions.

5. Talk about the experience. Ask: What materials do you think worked best for our containers? What was hard to use?

6. Bring a group of children together and have them dictate a group experience story about the water inventions. Let the children describe their own containers and how they worked.

Observing the Children

Are the children able to construct containers that hold water?

ACTIVITY 7

Flattening Play Clay

Materials

Play Clay

assorted devices for flattening clay, such as rolling pins, children's wooden hammers, and other unbreakable objects

interlocking cubes

What is the best tool to use to flatten Play Clay? Allowing the children to select different tools to try and discussing the results helps them to focus their attention on tools as a variable in performing a task.

Before the Activity

Make the Play Clay (see recipe on page 203) or use commercially available children's clay. Roll the clay into balls about the size of tennis balls. Make at least one clay ball per child. Flatten one of the clay balls.

What to Do

1. Show the children the two forms of Play Clay you created: the round ball and the flattened ball. Explain that you had to work to flatten the one ball.

C·O·N·N·E·C·T·I·O·N·S

To Language

Expressive Language - Children will use words to describe the action of their tools on their clay. They may use words such as *smash*, *squash*, *squeeze*, *pound*, and *smoosh*.

To Math

Measuring and Counting - Children will measure the width of their flattened clay with interlocking cubes and count the cubes.

Graphing - Children may make a whole-class graph showing how long the children's Play-Clay pieces were or how many used the same number of cubes.

Science Concept

Tools are made the way they are for specific purposes.

Science Process Skill

To focus observations by using the senses.

Science Vocabulary

change

flat, flatten

tool

tool names

2. Show the children the tools you have collected, and give each child a ball of Play Clay. Tell them that you want them to use these tools or others they find in the room to flatten their clay balls.

3. Say: When you have flattened your clay, come show it to me and tell me how you did it.

4. Have each child use interlocking cubes to measure the width of their flattened ball of clay. With the children, count the number of cubes.

5. As an optional activity, you could make a whole-class graph showing how long the children's Play-Clay pieces were or how many children's balls of clay measured the same width in terms of the number of cubes.

Observing the Children

The children should be able to describe the tools they used and how they did the activity.

ACTIVITY 8

Stamp-Pad Pictures

Materials

paper

washable stamp pads

variety of items that can be used to blot ink on paper, such as pieces of clay, potatoes, plastic foam, wood, brick, wax, and cardboard

paper towels (for clean up)

paper (for a Discovery Book)

If you did Art Center Activity 1, Litter Printing (page 232), the children explored objects that made useful tools in printing. Now they will focus on the classification of tools as effective or ineffective printers. You will have to

C•O•N•N•E•C•T•I•O•N•S

To Language

Expressive Language - As children make judgments about which objects make better stamps, they will use descriptive language to tell you why.

Discovery Book - Children will use their favorite stampers to make a class Discovery Book.

To Math

Comparing - Children will compare the two piles of objects and decide which has the most objects.

Science Concept

Tools are made the way they are for specific purposes.

Science Process Skill

To use observations to classify.

Science Vocabulary

absorb

group

print

stamp

first experiment with a number of materials before giving them to the children. After the printing experience, the children should be able to group the stampers by their being useful or not useful in printing.

What to Do

1. Encourage the children to investigate which materials are good ink stamps and which are not.

2. After all the children have had an opportunity to try the stamps, let them separate the stamps into good ink stamps and poor ones. Have the children compare the two piles and decide which has the most objects.

3. Ask the children if they can think of other materials and objects to try.

4. Let the children use their favorite stampers to make a class Discovery Book.

Observing the Children

Are the children able to separate materials into good ink stamps and poor ones?

ACTIVITY 1

A Sense of Balance

Materials

balance beam or a strip of tape or piece of string on the floor

unit blocks

paper and crayons (for a Discovery Book)

An interesting way to explore balance is to make a big "child size" walking balance. The balance beam can provide that experience and give the children a way to discover a sense of balance.

What to Do

1. Have the children try walking on the balance beam or tape line.

2. As the children walk the beam, use parallel talk to describe their actions, such as: "Look how she holds her arms as she walks." "You are using your arms to help keep your balance." "He's holding his arms out to help him balance on the beam." Have the children talk about what they do to keep their balance.

3. Have the children draw pictures of themselves or a friend on the balance beam. Put these pictures in a class Discovery Book.

C▪O▪N▪N▪E▪C▪T▪I▪O▪N▪S

To Language

Expressive Language - Children will talk about what they do to keep their balance.

Discovery Book - Children will draw pictures of themselves or a friend on the balance beam.

To Math

Measuring - Children will use their block balances to compare mass.

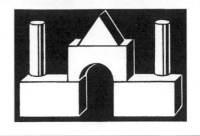

Science Concept

We can manufacture objects to allow us to accomplish certain tasks.

Science Process Skill

To focus observations by using the senses.

Science Vocabulary

balance

mass

4. After the children have learned to balance themselves on the balance beam, encourage them to explore ways they can use a long block and place it on another block that will act as a fulcrum and create a very simple balance. Ask: What happens when we put two blocks on the end of the long block? Yes, it goes down. What can we do to make it balance like you did when you walked on the beam?

5. Encourage the children to make additional balances using a variety of blocks. Crude though it may seem, challenge the children to use their block balances to compare mass. Ask them to balance an object you give them by placing blocks on the other side.

Observing the Children

Do the children demonstrate that they understand how to make things balance? Do they construct balanced block structures?

ACTIVITY 2

T 'Em Up

Materials

unit blocks

Building-block Ts offer another way for young children to explore balance. Encourage the children to experiment with bigger and taller constructions. Can they talk about what makes a structure fall?

What to Do

1. Show the children how to balance different shapes of blocks using an upright block as a support or T.

C•O•N•N•E•C•T•I•O•N•S

To Language

Expressive Language - Children will put their thoughts, actions, and the sequence of their actions into words.

To Math

Counting - Children may want to count how many Ts they have used.

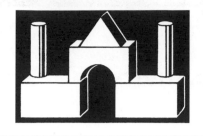

Science Concept

We can manufacture objects to allow us to accomplish certain tasks.

Science Process Skill

To focus observations by using the senses.

Science Vocabulary

balance

stack

support

2. Have the children experiment with different shapes of blocks, maybe even two or three blocks at a time.

3. Encourage the children to try supporting the blocks with two, three, or more Ts. Ask: Is it easier to add more blocks to the stack when you have more Ts? Encourage the children to build as big a structure as they can. They may want to count how many Ts they have used.

4. After children build their elaborate structures in the Block Center, encourage them to show their creations to you. By showing genuine interest and using questioning techniques that allow the children to focus on the building *process,* you can help the children put their thoughts, actions, and the sequence of those actions into words.

Observing the Children

Are children consistently able to create a balanced system within the limits of their individual fine-motor skills?

ACTIVITY 3

Rolling Along

Materials

unit blocks, including cylinders and long, flat blocks

long cardboard, plastic, or foam tubes

sturdy cardboard box

large sheet of newsprint and markers (for a Discovery Chart)

You can teach the children to use one of the simplest machines, the wheel, to do work. A heavy box can be moved easily with long cylinders. Ancient Egyptians built the pyramids using such contraptions. Let's see how the children use them.

What to Do

1. Have the children fill the cardboard box with blocks. Ask: Can you count the number of blocks you put in the box?

2. When the box is full, tell the children to move the box a few feet. Ask: How will you move it? Try it. They will probably try pushing or pulling the box.

3. Talk about how things move using items the children are familiar with such as wagons, cars, and tricycles. Help them focus on wheels. You might say: Yes, wheels help things move. They are round and they roll, which makes moving things much easier.

4. Say: Look at these blocks (a collection of long, round blocks and flat blocks). Do you see any that might make moving our box of blocks easier?

C ▪ O ▪ N ▪ N ▪ E ▪ C ▪ T ▪ I ▪ O ▪ N ▪ S

To Language

Discovery Chart - You will make a list of things that have wheels and carry things.

To Math

Counting - Children will count the number of blocks they place in the box.

Comparing - Children will compare the different cylinders that are good for moving the box.

Science Concept

Tools are made the way they are for specific purposes.

Science Process Skill

To focus observations by using the senses.

Science Vocabulary

cylinder

move

roll

roller

wheel

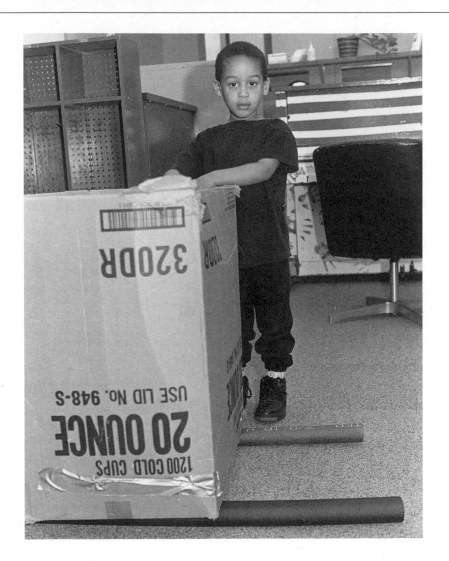

5. Say: Let us try putting these under the box to see if it will make moving the box easier. After the children have experimented with the cylinders, ask: Are any of the long, round blocks other round blocks for moving the box? Show the children how to work together to support the box as it moves so it doesn't fall onto someone's foot.

6. Encourage the children to try moving other things using rollers.

7. Have the children brainstorm all the things they can name that have wheels and carry things. List their ideas on a Discovery Chart, and add to it as children think of additional things.

Observing the Children

Do the children select the cylinders to assist in moving the box?

ACTIVITY 4

Ramps

Materials

plank, wide block of wood, or game board

blocks

selection of objects, some of which will roll, such as marbles, blocks, balls, checkers, dominos, pencils, jars, and rocks

The use of an inclined plane is standard practice in the physical sciences. This introduction to work and force, using a ramp as a tool, provides a very useful chunk of early learning. Ramps can be found many places in the real world: driveways, wheelchair access ramps, slanted floors in buildings, and escalators. Once the children experience the ramp, they will begin to see it everywhere.

What to Do

1. Build an incline plane with the children. Use blocks to adjust the height of the ramp.

2. Give the children the selected objects. Ask them to guess which objects they think will move down the ramp fastest.

3. Have the children test their guesses.

4. Emphasize comparative words such as *farthest, faster,* and *slow.* The children could collect the objects that traveled the farthest or fastest and place them in a winners' circle. They could then draw pictures of their favorites for you to caption.

C▪O▪N▪N▪E▪C▪T▪I▪O▪N▪S

To Language

Expressive Language - Children will use comparative words such as *farthest, faster,* and *slow.*

To Math

Measuring - Children may measure the distance objects traveled from the ramp.

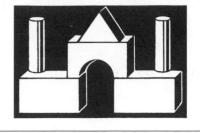

Science Concept

Tools are made the way they are for specific purposes.

Science Process Skill

To focus observations by using the senses.

Science Vocabulary

Comparative words such as farther, faster, slower

incline

ramp

roll

slant

slide

5. As an optional activity, have the children measure the distances objects travel using a simple unit such as a shoe. For example, the marble traveled eight shoes and the car traveled five shoes.

6. Send home How Objects Are Made and Used Family Connection Activity 1 (page 339).

Observing the Children

Can the children distinguish between the objects as they roll down the ramp using terms such as fast, slow, and faster?

ACTIVITY 5

Roller-Coaster Ride

Materials

standard pieces of 1-meter or 1-yard flexible foam pipe insulation, cut in half lengthwise

blocks

marbles

cups

boxes

masking tape

paper and crayons (for a Discovery Book)

In this activity, the children will be making a simple Rube Goldberg machine. They will need to experiment with the slope of inclined planes to get the marbles to move as they want them to move. With too steep a slope, the marbles may jump the track. If the slope is too level, the marbles may not go up the next hill.

What to Do

1. Show the children how to make various pathways for the marbles using blocks to create inclines. Construct a high incline and a low incline to compare how the marble rolls.

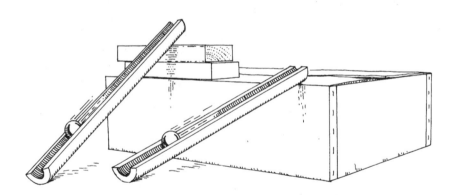

C▪O▪N▪N▪E▪C▪T▪I▪O▪N▪S

To Language

Discovery Book - Children will draw their roller coasters for a class Discovery Book.

To Math

Counting - Children will count the number of insulation units.

Comparing - Children will compare how the height and angle of the structure affect the speed of the marble.

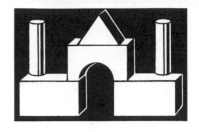

Science Concept

Tools are made the way they are for specific purposes.

Science Process Skill

To focus observations by using the senses.

Science Vocabulary

hill

ramp

roll

slope

2. The children can tape the structures to make them semi-permanent. They might create a path that ends with the marble splashing into a cup of water. Ask: Can you make a one-tube path? A two-tube path? A longer path?

3. Have the children roll marbles through their machines and describe what happens.

4. Have the children draw their roller coasters. Write down their words for them, and make a Discovery Book from the drawings and written descriptions.

Observing the Children

Do the children realize that a downhill slope is required for the marbles to roll?

ACTIVITY 6

Just a Little Longer

Materials

unit blocks

2 small chairs or tables

Building bridges in the Block Center provides children with simple estimation experiences. When you provide a space over which they must build and they choose the block to span it, they are estimating. With some practice, the children will begin to choose appropriate spans for each bridge.

What to Do

1. Place the two chairs or tables fairly close together so a short block will not bridge the gap but a longer block will. Have the children use a block to make a bridge between the two chairs. Encourage them to try several different blocks. Have them put the ones that make a bridge in one pile and those that do not in another pile.

C ▪ O ▪ N ▪ N ▪ E ▪ C ▪ T ▪ I ▪ O ▪ N ▪ S

To Language

Expressive Language - Children will use language to "think out" their predictions. Using comparative words such as shorter or longest will help them identify which blocks will work and which will not.

To Math

Comparing - Children will compare similarities of the blocks in each pile. They will determine which pile has more blocks.

Estimating - Children will estimate the length of a black needed to span the gap.

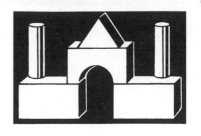

BLOCK CENTER

Science Concept

We can manufacture objects to allow us to accomplish certain tasks.

Science Process Skill

To use observations to classify.

Science Vocabulary

bridge

comparative words such as bigger, short, longest

measure

2. Select a block. Ask the children to guess if it is long enough to be a bridge across the two chairs.

3. Select another block. Ask the children how they might know if the block is not long enough without testing it across the gap. Can they compare its length to the blocks already tested and make an accurate prediction?

4. See if the children can look at the two piles and determine the similarity of the blocks in each pile. For example, they may say, "these are little blocks" or "these are the long ones." Have them select a block from each group and determine which is longer. Can they tell you which pile has more blocks?

5. When the children have had some experience with the block bridges, move the chairs a little farther apart. Which blocks that have already been tested will still work for this bridge?

Observing the Children

Are the children able to correctly identify blocks that are long enough to bridge the chairs?

ACTIVITY 1

Sieves and Sifters

Materials

sieve or strainer

colander or pasta strainer

paper cups in a variety of sizes

nails in a variety of sizes

marbles

water table or large, flat container filled with water

paper towels (for clean up)

In this activity, you provide children with a variety of containers that they use to create sieves and sifters—and to have fun experimenting.

What to Do

1. The word *sieve* will be unfamiliar to most of the children. Show the children the sieve and colander, and talk about how they work.

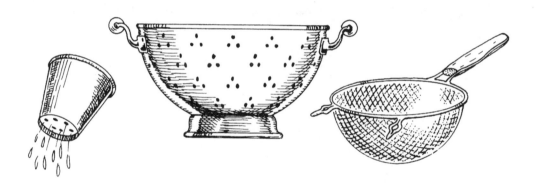

C·O·N·N·E·C·T·I·O·N·S

To Language

Expressive Language - Children will learn the word *sieve*.

To Math

Counting - Children will count the number of marbles they have caught in their cups.

Science Concept

We can manufacture objects to allow us to accomplish certain tasks.

Science Process Skill

To focus observations by using the senses.

Science Vocabulary

drain

poke

sieve

2. Show the children how to poke holes in the bottoms and sides of the cups with the nails to make sieves. Tell the children to turn the cup upside down and to *carefully* push the nail into the cup. Encourage them to try different cups and different sizes of nails.

3. Place several marbles on the bottom of the water table.

4. Demonstrate how the cups with holes can be used to pick up the marbles from below the surface of the water without holding any water. Hold up the cups to allow the water to drain through the holes, leaving the marbles in the cup. Ask: Can you count the number of marbles you catch in your cups? Talk about the ways that the different cups drain water, and the effect of the size and number of holes.

Observing the Children

Do the children understand that making more holes or larger holes makes for faster draining?

ACTIVITY 2

Sand Movers

Materials

toy machines (optional)

sand table or large, flat container filled with wet sand

objects that can be pushed through sand, such as blocks of wood, cups, and toy machines

Some tools are better than others for pushing sand around. A short, thin ruler will push sand, but not well. A big, wide board works very well, but may be too heavy for children to handle easily. Something will work just right for each child: just like Goldilocks said: This chair is *just* right. A tool may move just the right amount of sand and fit just right in the child's hands.

What to Do

1. Talk with the children about snow plows, road graders, and earth movers. You may want to bring in some toy machines to show them.

2. Show the children how to use a flat object to plow through the wet sand. Select another shape to plow through the sand. Ask: Does it work as well as the first object? Does one shape of earth mover work better than another shape?

C ▪ O ▪ N ▪ N ▪ E ▪ C ▪ T ▪ I ▪ O ▪ N ▪ S

To Language

Expressive Language - Children will use comparative language to discuss how the sand movers work and why some work better than others.

To Math

Comparing - Children will use comparative terms to indicate which objects moved the most sand.

SAND AND WATER CENTER

Science Concept

Tools are made the way they are for specific purposes.

Science Process Skill

To focus observations by using the senses.

Science Vocabulary

comparative words such as better, more

earth mover

grader

plow

shape

3. Ask the children to use blocks or other items to find which make good sand movers.

4. Now have the children look around the classroom to find other earth-moving things. When they have made their selections, let them experiment to find out which work well. What do they decide works the best?

5. Talk with the children about how the various sand movers work and why some work better than others. Ask: Which sand mover moved the most sand? The least?

Observing the Children

Do the children select earth movers that accomplish the task of moving the sand?

ACTIVITY 3

Water Movers

Materials

eye droppers

spoons

basters

straws

1-meter pieces of aquarium tubing

other water-moving materials, such as buckets, jars, basters, hoses, funnels and sponges

containers to hold water, such as plastic cups, tubs, and buckets

water table or large, flat container filled with water

paper towels (for clean up)

As in Sand and Water Center Activity 2, Sand Movers (page 262), some tools work better than others for moving water from one place to another. And certain tools work best for specific tasks. An eye dropper moves water precisely. A cup moves a greater volume than an eye dropper. Water Movers allows the children to learn for themselves the attributes of each tool.

What to Do

1. Draw the children's attention to the materials. Show them how you can use the cup to take water from the water table to move water to another container.

2. Show each of the other items that can be used to move water. Do not demonstrate how they work, but say that each can be used to move water from one container to another. Tell the children that their job is to figure out how that is done.

C ▪ O ▪ N ▪ N ▪ E ▪ C ▪ T ▪ I ▪ O ▪ N ▪ S

To Language

Expressive Language - Children will discuss which tool was the best water mover and why.

To Math

Counting - Children will count the number of times it takes a tool to transfer water from one container to another.

Comparing - Children will discuss which containers hold a lot of water and which hold a little water.

Science Concept

Tools are made the way they are for specific purposes.

Science Process Skill

To focus observations by using the senses.

Science Vocabulary

better, best, worst

little

tool names

3. Let the children experiment with the water movers. Help them discuss which tool is the best water mover and why.

4. Ask: Can you count the number of times it takes this tool to move water from one container to another? Which containers hold a little water? Which containers hold a lot of water?

Observing the Children

Are they able to use a variety of water-moving tools to transport water from one place to another?

ACTIVITY 4

Let's Make a Lake

Materials

story about a lake (optional)

sand table or large, flat container filled with sand

spoons

small shovels

plastic bags

containers to hold water

water

paper and crayons (for a Discovery Book)

paper towels (for clean up)

Turn the sand table into lake country! The children will enjoy planning, digging, and constructing lakes. They will explore water flow by experimenting with building dams and channels. You may be encouraging future civil engineers and community planners.

What to Do

1. Children can dig depressions in the sand to make a lake. You may or may not need to prompt them to do so. If the children are not familiar with lakes, you might want to read a story about a lake before the activity.

2. Have the children dig their holes and use the plastic bags to line some of the holes. Then have them fill their holes with water.

C▪O▪N▪N▪E▪C▪T▪I▪O▪N▪S

To Language

Discovery Book - Children will make a book about lakes using captioned drawings and their own scribble writing.

To Math

Counting and Measuring - Children may measure the volume of their lake by counting the number of cups it takes to fill it with water.

Science Concept

Tools are made the way they are for specific purposes.

Science Process Skill

To focus observations by using the senses.

Science Vocabulary

absorb

lake

liner

pond

soak

3. Encourage the children to experiment with various sizes of lakes. As they pour water into the lakes, they can observe and compare the flow of the water in the lined lakes with the flow in the unlined lakes. They will observe how the sand absorbs water and how the liner holds the water in.

4. As an optional activity, you could have children count the number of cups it takes to fill each lake with water. This can lead to a simple discussion about volume.

5. Make a Discovery Book about lakes using the children's captioned drawings and their own scribble writing. They may also want to include pictures of real lakes cut from magazines. If any of the children have visited a lake, include what they tell about it.

Observing the Children

Do the children understand that by placing plastic into the depressions they can make a lake and that by not using a liner the hole cannot hold water?

ACTIVITY 5

Plumber Apprentices

Materials

collection of plastic pipe in assorted lengths

variety of connectors

wrenches

tool box for connectors and wrenches

water table or large, flat container filled with water

containers to hold water

funnels

The plumber apprentices you will train during this activity will discover the complexities of a water line. The pieces will fit together and can be moved, allowing water to flow through. The children will see that interesting shapes will not always allow water to move through.

Before the Activity

Help yourself out by making a trip to a construction site or a plumbing store to ask for pieces of cast-off plastic pipe. Most people will be happy to save pieces for your class. Fittings and connectors, however, will probably have to be purchased.

What to Do

1. Place the materials in the Dramatic Play Center. Encourage the children to pretend being a plumber or a pipe fitter. They will enjoy constructing a variety of configurations.

C ▪ O ▪ N ▪ N ▪ E ▪ C ▪ T ▪ I ▪ O ▪ N ▪ S

To Language

Expressive Language - Children will expand their vocabulary as they learn words such as *elbow, T connector,* and *coupling.*

To Math

Comparing - Children will compare the various lengths of pipe and the types of connectors.

Science Concept

Tools are made the way they are for specific purposes.

Science Process Skill

To focus observations by using the senses.

Science Vocabulary

connector

names of connectors and plumbing tools

pipe

plumbing

2. After the children have had experience working with the pipes, encourage them to test their connections in the water table or outside. They can use the funnels to help pour water into the pipes.

3. Have the children compare the various lengths of pipe and the types of connectors.

4. Ask: Does the water come out where you expected it to come out? How could you make the water travel a different way? Is there a way you could attach more pieces? What is the longest distance you can make the water travel?

Observing the Children

Are the children able to successfully construct with the pipes and connectors?

ACTIVITY 6

Water Pressure

Materials

large plastic syringes

clear plastic aquarium tubing

water table or large, flat container filled with water

food coloring

paper towels (for clean up)

This activity allows the children to explore the principles of pressure in a closed system. They observe how pressure exerted on one part of a system causes change in another part of the system. Although they may never fully realize why the phenomenon takes place, they will be able to observe how pneumatic pressure devices work.

What to Do

1. Color the water in the water table with food coloring. Draw colored water into one of the two syringes. Connect the two syringes with a piece of plastic tubing.

2. Demonstrate to the children how, by pushing down on the plunger of the full syringe, the plunger of the empty syringe is pushed out. Even more interesting is that when the plunger of the empty syringe is pulled out, the full syringe's plunger is sucked in.

3. Place the materials in the water table for the children to explore. The children may need your guidance to learn how to move the plunger without pulling it out of the syringe.

C ▪ O ▪ N ▪ N ▪ E ▪ C ▪ T ▪ I ▪ O ▪ N ▪ S

To Language

Expressive Language - Children will use directional words, such as *in, out, up,* and *down.*

Science Concept

Tools are made the way they are for specific purposes.

Science Process Skill

To focus observations by using the senses.

Science Vocabulary

in, out

plunger

pressure

pull

push

syringe

up, down

Observing the Children

Are the children able to tell you what will happen when they move one of the plungers?

ACTIVITY 7

Help Me Fill This Up

Materials

plastic containers of varying sizes

water table

eye droppers

basters

funnels

sieves

syringes

measuring cups and spoons

water table or large, flat container filled with water

paper towels (for clean up)

Most jobs require specific tools and procedures. Sometimes one tool is better than another, and the reasons for that are obvious to the person performing the task. In this activity, the children are asked to choose the tool they feel is best suited to the task at hand.

What to Do

1. Place one of the containers at the water table along with the tools. By now the children should know how to use all the tools.

2. Say to one child: Can you fill up this container? Figure out which of these tools is best to put water in the jar. Do you want to do this job by yourself, or do you want some help?

3. Allow time for all the children to have a chance to work.

4. Add new containers of different sizes that will require different equipment to fill them. Ask individual children: Can you name this tool and describe how it works? You may want to give them a model such as, "This is a funnel. It does not hold water."

C▪O▪N▪N▪E▪C▪T▪I▪O▪N▪S

To Language

Expressive Language - Children will practice speaking in expanded sentences by stating a tool's name and describing how it works.

Science Concept

Tools are made the way they are for specific purposes.

Science Process Skill

To focus observations by using the senses.

Science Vocabulary

best, better

fill

names of tools used

tool

Observing the Children

Do the children select equipment that is appropriate for the size of container? Can they talk about why they chose the equipment they did?

ACTIVITY 8

Fill 'Er Up

This activity allows the children to differentiate between containers that hold water and those that do not. The children can also practice using important quantitative concepts such as *empty* and *full*.

Materials

several containers, some that hold water and some that do not

clear plastic cups

nail

water table or large, flat container filled with water

paper towels (for clean up)

Before the Activity

Use the nail to poke holes in the bottom of several plastic cups—one hole in the first, two in the second, three in the third, and so on. Make the holes near the bottom of the cups so the streams of water will flow separately.

What to Do

1. Encourage the children to investigate which containers hold water and which do not. Have them place the containers into two groups accordingly.

C ▪ O ▪ N ▪ N ▪ E ▪ C ▪ T ▪ I ▪ O ▪ N ▪ S

To Language

Expressive Language - Children will tell you which container takes longer to empty and why they have grouped the containers as they have. They will use the words *empty* and *full*.

To Math

Counting - Children will count the number of holes in the containers and the number of streams of water produced.

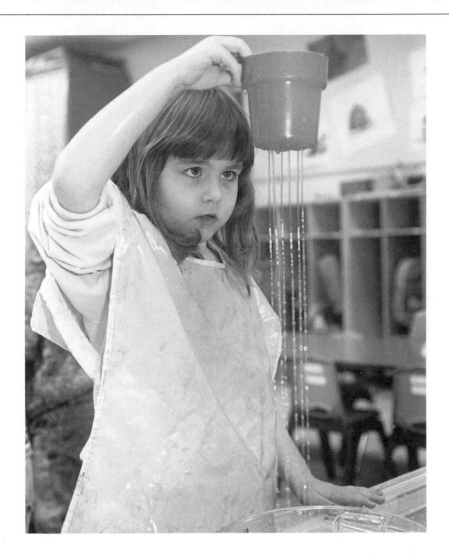

Science Concept

We can manufacture objects to allow us to accomplish certain tasks.

Science Process Skill

To use observations to classify.

Science Vocabulary

empty

full

stream

2. Show the children how the cup with one hole makes one stream of water. Have them try the cup with two holes. Ask: Is there a difference? Which takes longer to empty? What about three holes or four holes?

3. Have the children count the streams of water and count the holes. Are they the same?

Observing the Children

Select several different containers, ask the children to tell you whether they can hold water or not. Can the children order the cups by the number of streams of water they produce?

ACTIVITY 9

Sand-Table Mountains

Materials

set of funnels of various sizes

interlocking cubes

cups

sand table or large, flat container filled with sand

Building with sand is something nearly all children enjoy. They make mountains, castles, forts, and other things with wet sand. Dry sand responds much differently. This activity asks the children to make dry-sand mountains. Measuring adds a special skill to this building task.

What to Do

1. Demonstrate to the children how the funnel can be used to make sand mountains. Pour sand through the funnel as you hold it over the table.

2. Show them how to make a mountain-measuring ruler by joining interlocking cubes together and sticking this "ruler" in the sand table. Then pour sand through the funnel while holding it over the ruler.

3. Tell the children that their task is to produce the highest mountain of sand they can. While they work, help them use synonyms for *mountain* such as *hill, heap, pile,* and *mound.*

C ▪ O ▪ N ▪ N ▪ E ▪ C ▪ T ▪ I ▪ O ▪ N ▪ S

To Language

Expressive Language - Children will learn synonyms for *mountain.*

To Math

Graphing - Children will use the cube bar graph to compare the height of the mountains.

Science Concept

Tools are made the way they are for specific purposes.

Science Process Skill

To organize and communicate observations.

Science Vocabulary

funnel

graph

high, higher

measure

ruler

tall, taller

short, shorter

synonyms for mountain such as hill, heap, pile, mound

4. When the children have built their sand mountain to the greatest height possible, mark its height by removing the exposed cubes.

5. Pull the cube ruler out, and count its height with the children. Put the cube ruler aside. Allow each group of children a turn.

6. Use the cube rulers to create a three-dimensional bar graph that shows the relative heights of the sand mountains.

Observing the Children

Do the children relate high mountains to long lengths of cubes and short mountains to short lengths of cubes?

ACTIVITY 1

Pulleys

Materials

pulley (or a spool-and-coat-hanger pulley)

rope or clothesline

small bucket

assorted objects

labels or small squares of paper

crayons

This experience with a pulley introduces the children to one of the most important tools of physics. Later in their scientific training, they will learn more complex ways of using pulleys to do increasingly difficult jobs. Now is the time to explore ways to use a single pulley to do work in the block area.

Before the Activity

If you don't have access to a conventional pulley, you can construct one from a wire coat hanger and a spool. Cut the coat hanger along its bottom wire, insert the spool, and push together the wire ends to overlap them.

What to Do

1. Tie the rope to the bucket, and secure the pulley in such a manner that the children can pull down on the pulley's rope and raise the bucket off the floor.

C ▪ O ▪ N ▪ N ▪ E ▪ C ▪ T ▪ I ▪ O ▪ N ▪ S

To Language

Expressive Language - Children will use the concepts *up* and *down*.

Written Language - Children will "write" to create their own shipping labels for packages.

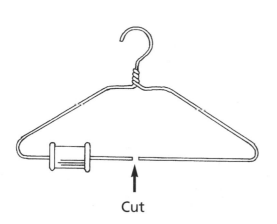

Cut

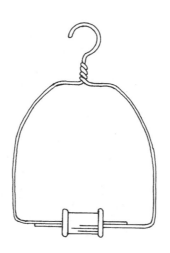

Science Concept

Tools are made the way they are for specific purposes.

Science Process Skill

To focus observations by using the senses.

Science Vocabulary

heavy

lift

pulley

up, down

wheel

2. Let the children discover how they can use the pulley system to lift blocks and other things. As the children work with the pulley, reinforce the concepts *up* and *down*. Encourage them to talk about whether picking up the bucket by hand is different from picking it up with the pulley.

3. Have the children "write" shipping labels for the packages being moved by the pulley by drawing on labels or pieces of paper.

Observing the Children

Are they able to manipulate the pulley successfully?

ACTIVITY 2

Balancing Junk

The dowel in this activity functions as a balance. The children will soon learn to estimate the relative masses of objects to create a balanced rod.

Materials

dowel rods

glue or tape

string

clothespins

variety of lightweight objects, such as paper cups and plates, pieces of plastic foam and fabric, cotton balls

Before the Activity

Tie a string to the center of each dowel and hold it in place with glue or tape. Suspend the rods within reach of the children. Tie a string from both ends of each dowel, and fasten a clothespin to each string. Take care that the rod assemblies do not slip.

What to Do

1. Demonstrate to the children how they can clip different objects to both sides of the rod until it is level or balanced. Let them work with the materials. The balance is a tool to weigh or compare objects. We are going to use a balance that we make.

C▪O▪N▪N▪E▪C▪T▪I▪O▪N▪S

To Language

Comparative Language - When discussing the activity, children will use words such as *up, down, heavy, light,* and *balance*.

To Math

Weighing and Comparing - Children will compare the masses of different objects.

Science Concept

Tools are made the way they are for specific purposes.

Science Process Skill

To focus observations by using the senses.

Science Vocabulary

balance

heavy, heavier

light, lighter

tool

up, down

2. Ask: How can you get one end of the rod to go up and the other end to go down? Can you make the rod even? Can you balance it? Give the children plenty of time to compare the relative masses of lots of different objects. With experience, they may begin to predict what will happen.

3. Use this activity to reinforce the concepts *up, down, heavy,* and *light.* You can also introduce the concept of *balance.*

Observing the Children

Can the children place objects on the clothespins to make the rod move the way they want to make it move?

ACTIVITY 3

Sticky Elbows

Materials

long-sleeve shirt

self-adhesive hook and loop fastener (such as Velcro®)

lightweight objects, such as small toys, nuts, wood scraps, and shells

This activity is a fun way to show children that some tools take more than one piece to work effectively. As they work with these special fasteners, they will discover that they need "two halves to make a whole."

Before the Activity

Prepare the shirt by putting a strip of a fastener pair on one of the elbows and the other side of the fastener on the other elbow. The elbows will attach to each other. Glue or attach fastener pairs to a variety of objects for the children to try to pick up. Each elbow will only work with items that have the opposite side of the fastener.

What to Do

1. Show the children the shirt with the special fastener on the elbows. Explain that they are going to be using a picking-up tool made with this fastener. Their job is to pick up objects that have a fastener strip attached to them. Demonstrate this.

2. Put opposite strips of fastener on each child's elbows as you did with your own shirt.

C▪O▪N▪N▪E▪C▪T▪I▪O▪N▪S

To Language

Expressive Language - Children will learn to use "right arm" and "left arm" to communicate which elbow was able to pick up which objects.

To Math

Grouping and Comparing - Children may group objects according to the arm that could pick them up. They may compare objects in the two groups.

Science Concept

We can manufacture objects to allow us to accomplish certain tasks.

Science Process Skill

To focus observations by using the senses.

Science Vocabulary

attach

left arm, right arm

lift

stick

3. Place the objects on a table in the Discovery Center. Allow the children to explore the objects and how they can be picked up.

4. Discuss with the children what happened as they used their new tools. Ask: Did one of your elbows pick up everything? Center the discussion around using a tool to do a certain task.

5. As an optional activity, have the children sort the objects into groups according to which arm was able to pick them up. The children can compare the objects in the two groups and talk about how they are alike and different (what half of fastener do they have?).

Observing the Children

Can the children tell you how the fastener works? They should be able to tell you that one type will pick up its opposite. From observation, they should be able to point out picking-up pairs.

ACTIVITY 4

Help Me Pick These Up

Materials

pick-up tools such as chopsticks, forceps, tweezers, spoons, barbecue tongs, and salad tongs

items to be picked up such as acorns, bolts, nuts, rocks, bricks, blocks, jars, and other containers

large box

This is another way for children to learn that different tools are designed for different purposes. Through their own trial and error, they will discover which tools are best suited to the task at hand.

What to Do

1. Place the tools on a table or on the floor, and place the items to be picked up beside them. Put the box on the table.

2. Explain to the children that their job is to use the tools to move the items from the table to the box (or to some other container, such as your cupped hand). They are to select a tool and see which things can be picked up with it and moved to the box. Encourage them to talk to each other as they move items to the box. They can announce when they have an object and tell others to clear the way so they can get to the box.

C ▪ O ▪ N ▪ N ▪ E ▪ C ▪ T ▪ I ▪ O ▪ N ▪ S

To Language

Expressive Language - Children will announce what they have done as they move objects.

To Math

Counting - Children will count the number of objects they are able to pick up and move.

Science Concept

Tools are made the way they are for specific purposes.

Science Process Skill

To focus observations by using the senses.

Science Vocabulary

forceps

pick up

pinch

squeeze

tongs

3. Have the children count the number of objects they are able to pick up and move. You may want to use a tally chart to keep track of their successes.

4. Send home How Objects Are Made and Used Family Connection Activity 2 (page 339).

Observing the Children

As the children are working, ask why they have chosen a particular tool and how it works to move the item. Ask the children to explain how they used the tools.

ACTIVITY 1

Clean Up a Spill

Materials

measuring cups

basters

squeegees

dust pans

plastic cup of water

plastic cup of sand

sponge, cloth, paper towels (for clean up)

This activity asks the children to respond to something that happens to us all. They are asked to try different equipment and reach their own conclusions as to what works best.

What to Do

1. Have the children sit in a circle. (The area used should have a tile or cement floor.) Place the collection of clean-up materials on the floor.

2. In the center of the circle, spill a plastic cup of water. Ask the children what should be done. The children will want to clean up the spilled water. Say: Choose some tools to help clean up the spill together.

3. When the clean up is complete, talk about how the different tools worked.

4. With the group, decide which of the tools did the best job of cleaning up the spill. Encourage the children to describe how the various tools work. You may need to provide words for their actions.

5. Repeat the activity using sand. Talk with the children about how different tools work better for different jobs.

C▪O▪N▪N▪E▪C▪T▪I▪O▪N▪S

To Language

Expressive Language - Children will talk about how the tools work and use terms such as *better* and *best* to describe the results.

Science Concept

Tools are made the way they are for specific purposes.

Science Process Skill

To focus observations by using the senses.

Science Vocabulary

clean up

names of tools

spill

Observing the Children

Are the children able to describe the tools that are most useful for cleaning up a certain type of spill?

ACTIVITY 2

Hammer, Hammer, What Do You Do?

This small-group activity lets children share what they have learned in a playful way. Be sure you work with small enough groups to allow for each child's active involvement.

Materials

eye droppers

basters

funnels

measuring cups

forceps

chopsticks

tongs

balls

bottles

rolling pin

sponge

rag

hammer

screwdriver

scissors

pliers

What to Do

1. Put the children in a circle around the items you have collected. Show them each of the materials. Ask the children to talk about how they used the materials in the activities they have done. Review how the eye dropper and the measuring cup were used to pick up water and move it from one place to another. The sponge and cloth picked up water, and the rolling pin was used for flattening clay. Go through everything. Add the hammer and screwdriver.

2. Give the children the following chant, practicing it with them until they can join you in the chant: "Hammer, Hammer what do you do? I bet (child's name) can tell you." With that, the child named should go over, pick up the hammer, and say, "A hammer is used to hit things." The child puts the hammer down and returns to his or her spot.

C ▪ O ▪ N ▪ N ▪ E ▪ C ▪ T ▪ I ▪ O ▪ N ▪ S

To Language

Expressive Language - Children will use language to describe actions.

Science Concepts

Tools are made the way they are for specific purposes.

We can manufacture objects to allow us to accomplish certain tasks.

Science Process Skill

To organize and communicate observations.

Science Vocabulary

names of tools

3. Continue the activity. For example, say: "Pliers, pliers what do you do? I bet (child's name) can tell you." The next child named walks into the center, picks up the pliers, and tells what it does.

4. Go through all the objects, giving each child a turn. This activity encourages the children to use language to describe actions. Let children who do not have the words show how the tools are used. You can supply the words to describe their actions.

Observing the Children

Can the children either verbalize or show you how the tools are used?

ACTIVITY 3

Knock It Over

Materials

several 1-liter and 2-liter bottles

sand

balls, blocks, and other objects to knock the bottles over

poster board

markers

This activity gives children the opportunity to work with various combinations of objects to find what works best for them. In the process, they learn to play a fun game.

What to Do

1. Fill the bottles with different amounts of sand. Place the bottles upright in a triangle as one would see them in a bowling alley. Show the children the objects that might be used to knock the bottles over.

2. Explain to the children that they are to determine what combination of bottles and objects would work best to knock down the bottles.

3. Demonstrate the bowling procedure. Show the group how the bottles have been filled differently.

C ▪ O ▪ N ▪ N ▪ E ▪ C ▪ T ▪ I ▪ O ▪ N ▪ S

To Language

Comparative Language - Children will describe how and why some bottles are harder to knock over than others.

To Math

Data Collection and Analysis - Children will make a large chart to show the number of bottles they knock over.

Science Concept

Tools are made the way they are for specific purposes.

Science Process Skill

To organize and communicate observations.

Science Vocabulary

bowling

easy, hard

heavy, heavier

light, lighter

4. Let the children use the various objects to try and knock over the bottles. Afterward, talk about what happens.

5. Use the poster board to make a large chart for the children to mark an X in a square for each bottle they knock over.

Observing the Children

The children should be able to tell which of the bowling objects worked best to knock down the bottles.

Jorge	Sue	Noah	Nari
x	x	x	X
X	X	X	x
x	x		X
	X		

ACTIVITY 1

Feather Wind Gauge

Materials

string

small turkey or chicken feathers

tape or glue

large sheet of newsprint and markers
(for a Discovery Chart)

Wind direction and velocity are important weather information given to us each day on the news report. The children, too, can determine the direction wind moves by using a simple weather vane as a tool.

What to Do

1. Help the children tie a piece of string to the quills of the feathers and attach it using tape or glue.

2. Demonstrate what the feather will do on a windy day by holding it out and blowing. To demonstrate a still day, hold the feather out and do not blow.

3. Hang the wind gauges in an accessible spot. When the children go on a walk or whenever they please, have them determine if it is a still or a windy day.

C ∙ O ∙ N ∙ N ∙ E ∙ C ∙ T ∙ I ∙ O ∙ N ∙ S

To Language

Expressive Language - Children will describe how the wind moves the wind gauge using the science vocabulary words.

Discovery Chart - You will make a chart listing windy and still days.

To Math

Graphing - Children may mark the number of windy days and still days over a given period on the daily calendar.

Science Concept

We can manufacture objects to allow us to accomplish certain tasks.

Science Process Skill

To focus observations by using the senses.

Science Vocabulary

blow

calm

fast, slow

hard, gentle

still

storm words

tool

wind

4. If it seems appropriate, note the direction from which the wind blows. Does that direction change from day to day, or is it constant?

5. With the children, make a Discovery Chart listing windy and still days. You may want to mark the number of windy and still days over a given period on the daily calendar.

Observing the Children

The children should be able to use the wind gauges as tools to tell whether the wind is blowing. Some might be able to look out on a windy day and predict that the feather wind vane will move today.

ACTIVITY 2

Birds Like to Eat, Too

Materials

aluminum pie plates

variety of seeds, such as sunflower seeds, thistle seeds, and mixed bird-seed

Few things can take the place of a bird feeder for keeping the children interested in outdoor wildlife. Bird feeders can be located almost anywhere to attract some of our little feathered friends. This activity lets the children make a tool that can provide months of enjoyment for the entire class.

What to Do

1. Talk to the children about things they like to eat. Ask: When do you usually eat? What do you eat? Do birds like to eat as much as we do? When we eat, we usually come to the table where food is served. We can make a place for birds to come to eat. The place is called a bird feeder.

2. Place the pie plates outside, making sure that they are visible from your windows.

C▪O▪N▪N▪E▪C▪T▪I▪O▪N▪S

To Language

Expressive Language - Children will use color and size to describe the birds they see. You may want to provide specific names for the types of birds and birdseed.

To Math

Counting - Children will count how many birds are at the feeder at a given time.

Comparing - Children will compare the types of birds that come to the feeder.

Science Concept

We can manufacture objects to allow us to accomplish certain tasks.

Science Process Skill

To focus observations by using the senses.

Science Vocabulary

bird

bird names

seed names

tool

3. Put seeds in the pie plates. You may want to mix seeds in some of the feeders and place only one type of seed in others.

4. Let the children observe the various birds and the kinds of foods that attract them. Ask: How long do the birds stay? Is there a certain type of bird that comes to the feeder most often? How many come to the feeder at a time? How many people come to your table when you eat dinner?

Observing the Children

The children should come to understand that birds need to eat just as we do.

ACTIVITY 3

Find a Lion—A Pretty, Yellow Dandelion

Materials

dandelion removing tool or garden trowel

The dandelion is a wonderful tool for exploring the parts and states of a plant. They have a large tap root, no stem, many leaves, and a distinct flower and seed arrangement. The dandelion is a composite flower that belongs to the same group as the sunflower and daisy. And they grow everywhere.

What to Do

1. Explore a nearby grassy area for dandelions. Show the children a dandelion with flowers, flower buds, and flowers that have gone to seed.

2. Talk about how flowers grow old just like people. They are young, grow old and change, and finally die.

3. Show the children how to use the dandelion tool to uproot several plants in various stages of growth.

C▪O▪N▪N▪E▪C▪T▪I▪O▪N▪S

To Language

Expressive Language - Children will use color words and other language to talk about the bud, flower, and seed head of the dandelion.

To Math

Matching - Children will match the plants in three stages of development.

Science Concept

Tools are made the way they are for specific purposes.

Science Process Skill

To use observations to classify.

Science Vocabulary

bud

dandelion

flower

leaf

root

seeds

tap root

tool

weed

4. Have the children look at the plants very carefully. Point out the different stages of the flowers, from very young buds to those that have shed their seeds. Talk about the tap root. Do they remember seeing tap roots earlier? See if the children can put the plants together according to their stages of development.

Observing the Children

The children should be able to match plants from three stages of the dandelion life cycle.

ACTIVITY 4

Sounds Around Us

Materials

tape recorder

tally sheet

clipboard

large sheet of newsprint and markers
(for a Discovery Chart)

While out on the school grounds, you can help the children explore the world of outdoor sound. Bird watchers often do not see all the birds they are observing, but rely on the sounds the birds make to count the birds. Seeing in the outdoors is important, but so is listening.

What to Do

1. Take the children on a listening walk. This can be done in a rural area or in the city. Encourage them to describe the sounds. Talk about loud sounds, pretty sounds, annoying sounds, distant sound, sounds from animals, and sounds from machines.

2. Make frequent stops on the walk. Tell the children you want them to be very still and to listen to the sounds around them. Capture these sounds on a tape recorder. After a minute or so, pause to let the children tell you what they have heard.

C▪O▪N▪N▪E▪C▪T▪I▪O▪N▪S

To Language

Expressive Language - Children will identify the sounds they hear.

Discovery Chart - You will list the sounds the children remember and their sources.

To Math

Classifying - Children think of ways to group the sounds.

Tally Sheet - The children will assist you in making a tally sheet to record the sounds.

Science Concept

Tools are made the way they are for specific purposes.

Science Process Skill

To organize and communicate observations.

Science Vocabulary

ear

hear

listen

record

sound

sound source names

3. Return to the classroom. List the sounds the children can remember from their walk on the Discovery Chart. List both the sound and the source of the sound, if they know what it is.

4. Listen to the sounds again as you play back the tape. Ask: Can you tell me what you hear now? Are there any sounds you do not recognize? Add any new sounds to the Discovery Chart.

5. While reviewing the Discovery Chart, ask: How many way can you think of to group the sounds?

Observing the Children

The children should be able to distinguish some of the sounds captured on tape. They might name what made the sound or tell where they were when they heard it. They will also recognize the tape recorder as a tool to collect and record the sounds in their environment.

ACTIVITY 5

The Measurement Walk

Materials

interlocking cubes or other measuring devices

graph paper

crayons

Interlocking cubes are useful tools to introduce the skill of measurement to the children. And in the outdoors, an array of plants exists for observing and measuring.

What to Do

1. Take a group of children on a measuring walk. Find a plant—not too large—and measure it using the cubes. You will have to work with the children to place the cubes on the ground and build the stack to the height of the plant.

2. When you have measured several plants, help the children use the stacks of cubes to determine the tallest and shortest plant measured. If they can, let the children count the number of cubes used. Ask: Are some plants the same height? How can you tell?

C•O•N•N•E•C•T•I•O•N•S

To Language

Expressive Language - Children will use comparative language such as *tallest, shortest, same,* and *little* to describe the plants.

To Math

Measuring - Children will use simple measurement to compare the height of plants.

Counting - Some of the children will be able to count the number of cubes used.

Science Concept

Tools are made the way they are for specific purposes.

Science Process Skill

To organize and communicate observations.

Science Vocabulary

comparative language such as tallest, shortest

measure

plant

plant names

tool

3. Using graph paper, let the children take turns coloring in one square for each cube used to measure the plants.

Observing the Children

Can the children put the cubes together to make the measurement? Can they identify the tallest and shortest plants? Do they recognize that the cubes can be used as measurement tools?

ACTIVITY 6

Maps: Where We've Been and Where We're Going

Materials

large sheet of newsprint or butcher paper

tape

glue

markers

This activity introduces children to maps. They begin to understand that maps are tools that can be used as sources of information about location, distance, and physical features. In this case, the map is of the school yard, and the children will help collect information and place it on the map.

What to Do

1. As the children watch, make a map of the school yard. Be sure to draw it with the same orientation as the buildings. Draw in the buildings, sidewalks, play areas, trees, shrubs, and other large objects. Use relationship and position terms such as *up, below, under,* and *next to* as you create the map. Say things such as: What goes next to the slide? Talk about how the map is a drawing or model of your school yard. Ask: Has anyone seen a map being used when the family goes for a drive?

C▪O▪N▪N▪E▪C▪T▪I▪O▪N▪S

To Language

Expressive Language - Children will use relationship terms as they use the map.

To Math

One-to-One Correspondence - As the children look at the map outside, they will match the drawings to the real places.

Comparing - Children will be introduced to the idea of scale by comparing the little map to the big school yard.

Science Concept

Tools are made the way they are for specific purposes.

Science Process Skill

To organize and communicate observations.

Science Vocabulary

map

relationship terms such as up, below, under, next to

tool

2. Take the children on a mapping expedition to locate objects around the school yard. While on the adventure, follow the map. Allow each child to collect one object from the walk. Each child is to remember where the item was found. Cover the entire yard. Introduce the idea of *scale* by talking about how the little map is a drawing of the big school yard.

3. Return to the classroom, and have each child tell what he or she found and where it was collected. With your help, have them locate the collection site on the map. Tape or glue the objects on the map.

4. Continue until each child has a turn.

5. Share your school-yard map with parents. Suggest they repeat this activity at home by mapping their own yard.

Observing the Children

Can the children point out common objects on the map?
Do they recognize the map as a model of the school yard?
Can they find the place to add their materials?

ACTIVITY 7

Animal Watchers

Materials

empty toilet paper rolls

masking tape

clipboard and tally sheet

large sheet of newsprint and markers
(for a Discovery Chart)

An animal walk is an excellent way to gather information about the many animals present in the children's environment. This activity allows the children to focus on specific animals as they locate, identify, and count those they see on their journey.

What to Do

1. Assist the children as they make binoculars using two empty toilet-paper rolls and a strip of masking tape.

2. Ask the children what kinds of animals they saw on the way to school this morning. They might have seen a squirrel, a dog, or a cat.

3. Say: Today we are going to take a walk. We will use our binoculars to see how many different kinds of animals we can spot.

4. Take the walk. Remind the children that it is important to walk quietly so as not to disturb or scare the animals away. Say: When you spot something, tell me what you think it is. You might see birds, dogs, cats, insects, squirrels, cattle, or horses.

C ▪ O ▪ N ▪ N ▪ E ▪ C ▪ T ▪ I ▪ O ▪ N ▪ S

To Language

Expressive Language - Children will describe the animals they see.

Discovery Chart - You will list the animals the children see on their walk and descriptions of the animals.

To Math

Comparing - Children will compare the numbers of different kinds of animals.

Science Concept

We can manufacture objects to allow us to accomplish certain tasks.

Science Process Skill

To organize and communicate observations.

Science Vocabulary

animal names, such as insect, worm, bird, dog, sparrow

binoculars

tool

wildlife

5. Keep a tally of animals the children see on the walk. Help them expand their uses of descriptive language by providing new vocabulary as you talk together. On subsequent walks, make comparisons about what they see this time that is different from their last experience.

6. Upon returning to the classroom, talk about the animals the children spotted, using the list as a reference. Make a Discovery Chart to record what the children say about the various animals. Add to the Discovery Chart in another color as they tell you about other animals they see during subsequent walks. You may want to make another chart about the children's pets.

Observing the Children

The children should be able to identify by name the common animals they observe. They should recognize the use of the tally sheet as a tool to record data. When seeing a new animal, they should ask you to record its name and location.

ACTIVITY 8

How Much Did It Rain?

Materials

margarine tubs, coffee cans, or assorted containers

interlocking centimeter cubes (optional)

Rain can be a nuisance or a learning tool. In this lesson, rain and the trip to the school yard to check the results provide a focus on a natural occurrence. If you live in a geographical area where there is little rain, measurement may be out, but children may still be able to collect rain and hold it in their hands.

What to Do

1. On a day or an evening with a rain forecast, let the children place containers in open areas around the school yard.

2. After the rain has fallen, have the children go to each container and observe the depth of the water. If lots of rain has fallen, you might want to have the children measure the amount of rain with interlocking cubes.

3. As the children compare the containers, see whether they notice that the depth is the same in all of the containers.

C · O · N · N · E · C · T · I · O · N · S

To Language

Expressive Language - Children will share their experiences with and feelings about rain storms.

To Math

Comparing - The children will be able to compare the depths of the water.

Science Concept

We can manufacture objects to allow us to accomplish certain tasks.

Science Process Skill

To organize and communicate observations.

Science Vocabulary

deep, deeper

depth

measure

rain, rainfall

shallow, shallower

weather

4. This activity gives you the opportunity to talk with the children about rain and storms—frightening experiences for some children. Encourage the children to share their experiences and feelings.

Observing the Children

Do the children realize that the rain filled all the containers to the same depth?

PROP BOXES FOR SCIENCE CAREERS

Young children understand and learn about their world through play. Creative dramatic play offers an opportunity for them to imagine themselves in important adult roles. Through their imaginations, they can become in play what they cannot yet be in real life.

Prop boxes are boxes that contain real materials used by people in specific science professions. The children will enjoy using the objects as they act out roles. Through their play they will have many opportunities to express themselves as they develop awareness of the many science professions. Some of the science careers you may want to make prop boxes for include the following:

Archaeologist	Gardener or Horticulturist
Astronaut or Mission	Museum Curator
Control Specialist	Optometrist or Ophthalmologist
Astronomer	Pharmacist
Aviator	Trash Collector or Recycler
Botanist	Veterinarian
Chemist	Zoologist
Forest Ranger	

Constructing Prop Boxes

Begin with a sturdy box large enough to hold a number of props, yet small enough for the children to handle. Containers other than boxes can be used to emphasize a theme; for example, a doctor's bag, a geologist's sack, or a paleontologist's backpack.

Label each box with the name of the science occupation for which the props are intended. Let the children decorate the boxes with their drawings or with pictures cut from magazines.

Use parents, friends, professionals, and yard sales to collect items for the boxes. Since many professions use the same tools and props, it may be necessary to have a series of boxes with items common for many roles. Related books and cassette tapes can enhance the imaginative play initiated by the objects.

Put a card in each box that lists the items in the box. By checking this card after the boxes are used, you will be able to keep the materials organized and know when to replenish consumables.

Using Prop Boxes

You may want to use prop boxes in the Dramatic Play Center, the Discovery Center, or any other area in the room. They may also be used outdoors. Some discussion about the materials and their uses will probably be necessary before the children begin their play. If there are safety concerns, share these as well. Allow the children to play freely. If you join in the play, be an enthusiastic partner, but do not direct the action. Your role is that of an observer and as a recorder of children's actions, reactions, and discussions.

SAMPLE PROP BOX 1

Science Profession Theme: FORESTER, FOREST RANGER, SMOKE JUMPER

Resources for Acquiring Materials: horse owners, campers, scouts, Department of Conservation, county map offices, National Wildlife Federation, other naturalist groups

Contents:

- aerial survey map
- assorted animal artifacts for park education, such as deer antlers, a hoof, and a beaver jaw
- assorted literature available from state park offices (for children to pretend to give to park visitors)
- beeper
- binoculars
- catalog with forestry supplies and sample order forms (for children to pretend to order supplies)
- chain saw
- child-size rake (for forest fires)
- child-size shovel
- compass
- empty orange spray-paint can (for marking trees to be removed)
- envelopes and paper (for children to pretend to send letters to landowners about selling trees)
- hard hat
- hard hat with light
- saddlebag
- leaf collection
- magnifying glass
- orange trail-marking flags
- orange plastic tape (for marking trees)
- plastic or fabric tape measure
- riding boots
- cross sections of trees (for observing rings)
- seedlings, pinecones, and acorns
- sliding rule (for measuring trees)
- Smokey the Bear posters
- walkie-talkie
- water
- work boots
- yardstick or meter stick (for measuring trees)

Books, Records, Tapes:

Project Learning Tree K–6 by the American Forest Institute. Washington, D.C.: 1977.
I Can Be a Forest Ranger by C. Greene. Chicago: Children's Press, 1989.
My Dad's a Smokejumper by M. Hill. Chicago: Children's Press, 1977.
My Dad's a Park Ranger by M. Hill. Chicago: Children's Press, 1977.
The Tree by G. Jeunesse and C. Broutin. New York: Scholastic, 1992.
Trees Are Terrific! by the National Wildlife Federation Staff. Washington, D.C.: National Wildlife Federation, 1991.
Hug a Tree by R. Rockwell, E. Sherwood, and R. Williams. Mt. Rainier, Md.: Gryphon House, 1982.

Notes/Comments:

(Use this space for recording ideas or responses that occur as a result of using the prop box.)

_____

_____

_____

_____

Adapted with permission from Pam Cline, Collinsville, Illinois Unit 10 Pre-K Program.

SAMPLE PROP BOX 2

You may want to put this in a black doctor's bag.

DOCTOR

Science Profession Theme: DOCTORS OR HOSPITAL PERSONNEL

Resources for Acquiring Materials: hospitals, doctors, nurses, medical associations, health department

Contents:

bandages
bandage tape
bedpan
charts
cotton swabs
doctor gowns
dressings
eye charts
eye droppers
finger splints
flashlight
foam headrest
foot covers
gauze sponges
masks

medicine containers
medicine cups
note pads
patient gowns
reflex hammer
rubber gloves
scissors
stethoscope
surgeon's cap and bonnets
syringes (no needles)
tongue depressors
tubing
tweezers
X rays

Books, Records, Tapes:

One Bear in the Hospital by C. Bucknall. New York: Dial Books for Young Readers, 1991.
Curious George Goes to the Hospital by H. A. Rey and M. Rey. Boston: Houghton Mifflin, 1973.

Notes/Comments:

(Use this space for recording ideas or responses that occur as a result of using the prop box.)

_____

_____

_____

_____

_____

_____

_____

THE FAMILY CONNECTION

This section includes complete plans for organizing and running two Discovery Science Family Nights to introduce families to the Discovery Science curriculum, philosophy, goals, and activities.

The first meeting is designed to introduce the curriculum and to show how it will be implemented in the preschool environment. The activities at this meeting will also heighten families' science awareness and show them what three- and four-year-olds are developmentally able to do as the natural scientists they are. The second meeting, held six weeks later, will focus on the importance of the parents' and teachers' roles as partners in facilitating an environment that supports active discovery. The success of your Family Night science activities could lead to other events and activities.

At the end of this section are samples of letters inviting families to participate in the Family Connection activities. These activities can be sent home with children to extend their science experiences. For each Family Connection activity, put the materials called for and a photocopy of the instructions in resealable plastic bags.

Discovery Science Family Night: First Meeting

Dear Family,

This year we will be using a program designed to introduce your child to the exciting world of science. The program is called Discovery Science. It enables the children to learn science through discovery— through interactions with materials in their everyday environment at home, at school, and in the world. They will be learning science the way we all learn best: by doing, exploring, asking questions, and finding answers.

This is your invitation to come and learn what Discovery Science is all about and how we plan to include it in our curriculum. The meeting will last for about two hours. You will have the opportunity to try many of the activities the children will be doing over the next year. By the close of the meeting, you will have an understanding of the philosophy, goals, and activities of Discovery Science. You will also know your three- or four-year-old will be learning science in a developmentally appropriate way.

We want you to be comfortable, so please dress casually. The meeting will start and finish on time. We will have refreshments. Because this is an "adults only" meeting, child care will be provided. We will supply transportation if needed.

The meeting will be held at _____ on _____ from
_____ to _____. If you are able to attend, please return the bottom portion of this letter. Let us know how many adults will be coming and whether you will need child care.

We look forward to doing Discovery Science with you.

Sincerely,

Please Detach and Return by _____

_____ adults will attend the Discovery Science meeting.

_____ children, ages _____, will need child care.

Transportation needed?   Yes   No

We can provide transportation for another family.   Yes   No

Name _____

Phone _____

Reminder Flier

DON'T FORGET!

YOU ARE INVITED TO A DISCOVERY SCIENCE FAMILY MEETING

REFRESHMENTS WILL BE SERVED

CHILD CARE WILL BE PROVIDED

DATE: _____

TIME: _____

PLACE: _____

Please reserve two hours. This will be an excellent chance for you to discover Discovery Science, the exciting new science curriculum we are introducing this year. You will be able to take part in activities that will enable your children to develop their natural science abilities as they interact with materials in the environment of our center.

Name Tag and Mixer

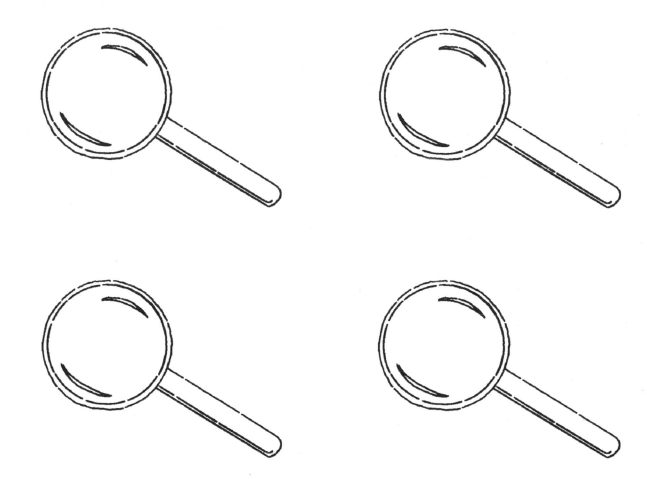

MIXER PROCEDURE

Trace the name tag pattern on construction paper and cut out the magnifying glasses. Write a number from 1 to 4 on the back of each name tag. This number will be used to assign each family member to one of the four interest centers: How Objects Are Alike and Different, How Objects Move, How Objects Change, and How Objects Are Made and Used. Set up these centers in open areas that will accommodate the materials and numbers of people attending. Gather the items for the scavenger hunt (listed below). Put several items in a bag, one bag for each guest.

As people arrive, hand each a name tag, a pin, and the bag of a collection of science items. Ask that they write their name on the tag, pin it on, and be seated.

After all the people have arrived, distribute the Discovery Science Scavenger Hunt Checklist. (Change the items if you can't locate some of these; use duplicate items if many people are expected.) Explain that you want them to stand, move around the room, and interact with one another while trying to find people who have objects on the checklist. Tell them that they should try to collect a different person's signature for each discovery item.

Discovery Science Scavenger Hunt Checklist

DISCOVER SOMEONE WHO HAS   SIGNATURE

1. acorn   _____

2. walnut   _____

3. hickory nut   _____

4. pine cone   _____

5. kernel of corn   _____

6. various shells   _____

7. magnet   _____

8. feather   _____

9. chicken bone   _____

10. owl pellet   _____

11. pumpkin seed   _____

12. seaweed   _____

13. magnifier box   _____

14. meal worm   _____

15. snake skin   _____

16. snail fossil   _____

17. animal tooth   _____

18. pearl tapioca   _____

19. pipette   _____

20. tree bark   _____

21. tree cookie   _____
    (*slice of a branch showing rings*)

Sample Agenda for Planning the First Family Night

Purpose: To introduce families to the Discovery Science curriculum, philosophy, goals, and activities.

Three Weeks Before Meeting

1. Clear meeting date with the center director.
2. Secure authorization for building and room use.
3. Secure a room for child care.
4. Make arrangements for several child-care providers to be on standby. Need will depend on the number of children that will be brought.
5. Select a transportation committee chairperson to make arrangements for families who need rides.
6. Select a refreshment committee chairperson. Post a sign-up sheet where families have access to it as they drop off and pick up their children.
7. Ask for volunteers or staff members to assist at the interest centers. They will explain procedures to families.

Two Weeks Before Meeting

1. Prepare and send invitations.
2. Lay out the physical arrangement of the meeting room on paper.
3. Decide which Discovery Science activities will be used in each of the interest centers.
4. Choose one or two activities for each center.

One Week Before Meeting

1. Prepare name tags.
2. Prepare Discovery Science Scavenger Hunt bags and checklists.
3. Prepare evaluation form and make copies.
4. Check with refreshment committee chairperson. Remind families of foods they have signed up to bring.
5. Send home a reminder flier with each child.
6. Check with the transportation committee chairperson to see if all who need rides are accommodated.

One Day Before Meeting

1. Send home final reminder.
2. Check progress of the refreshment committee. Get a final head count.
3. Verify that you have enough child-care providers for the age and number of children coming, and remind child-care providers of the time of the meeting.
4. Check with the transportation committee chairperson to verify rides for families needing them.

5. Check with the refreshment committee chairperson to touch base on arrangements.

6. Locate a bell, small alarm, or timer to use to tell people when to move to the next activity.

Day of Meeting

1. Set up chairs. Set up interest centers with one or two Discovery Science activities for each of the centers. Mark the centers 1–4.

2. Put up signs directing families to the meeting location.

3. Place name tags, pins, pens or pencils, and Scavenger Hunt bags and checklists on a table near the entrance to the room. Have evaluation forms handy.

Sample Discovery Science Meeting Plan

Time	Activity	Technique	Resources/Materials
7:00–7:10	Greeting	Greet families as they arrive. Hand out name tags, pins, and Scavenger Hunt bags.	Name tags, pins, pencils or pens, and bags containing science collections.
7:10–7:20	Mixer	Introduce and begin Scavenger Hunt.	See page 317 for mixer procedure.
7:20–7:30	Welcome participants. Introduce Discovery Science curriculum and explain centers.	Mini-lecture. Welcome families. Introduce Discovery Science curriculum and interest centers. Explain that people will go to the center matching the number on the name tag. When the bell rings, they will rotate clockwise to the next center. There will be one or two Discovery Science activities at each of the four stations.	Introduction to Discovery Science, pages 1–13.
7:30–8:30	Family members go to four centers.	Family members interact with materials at each center. A staff member or volunteer at each center can explain procedures and assist with the activities.	Four interest centers: How Objects Are Alike and Different, How Objects Move, How Objects Change, and How Objects Are Made and Used.
8:30–8:45	Reassemble into large group.	Wrap up. Hand out copies of "What Is Discovery Science?"	Handout: "What Is Discovery Science?" (page 322).
8:45–9:00	Closing Evaluation Refreshments	Hand out evaluation forms; serve refreshments; invite families to the next meeting.	Evaluation forms, pencils or pens.

What Is Discovery Science?

DISCOVERY SCIENCE IS

Your child exploring the natural world.

Your child beginning to use the tools of science.

Your child learning to ask questions and to look for answers.

Your child being involved in hands-on learning.

Your child having fun.

Discovery Science Needs You!

What Is Discovery Science?

DISCOVERY SCIENCE IS

Your child exploring the natural world.

Your child beginning to use the tools of science.

Your child learning to ask questions and to look for answers.

Your child being involved in hands-on learning.

Your child having fun.

Discovery Science Needs You!

Discovery Science Family Meeting Evaluation Form

We are interested in knowing whether you enjoyed the meeting this evening. Please circle the magnifying glass that best describes your understanding about the theory behind Discovery Science. The space at the bottom of this page is for questions or suggestions you have. We value your feedback, so please feel free to comment.

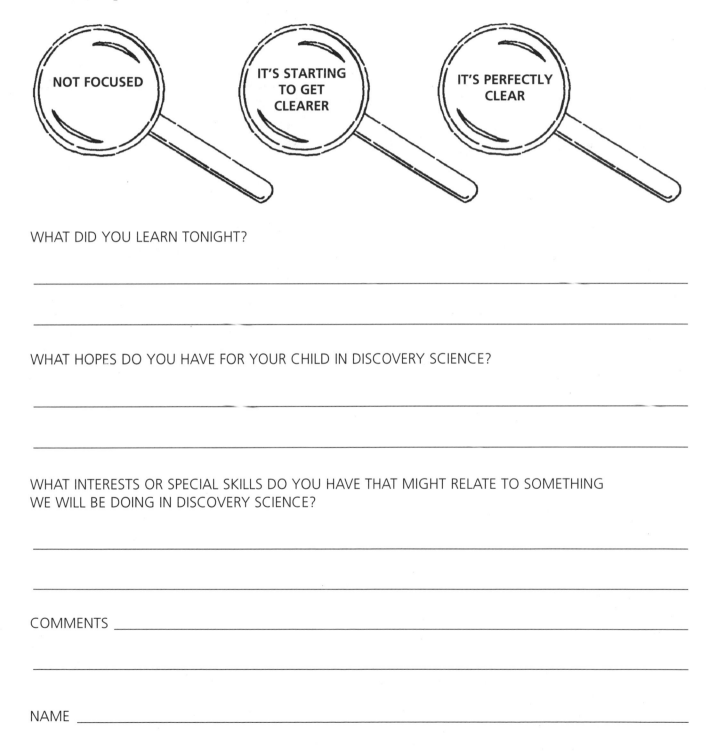

WHAT DID YOU LEARN TONIGHT?

_____

_____

WHAT HOPES DO YOU HAVE FOR YOUR CHILD IN DISCOVERY SCIENCE?

_____

_____

WHAT INTERESTS OR SPECIAL SKILLS DO YOU HAVE THAT MIGHT RELATE TO SOMETHING
WE WILL BE DOING IN DISCOVERY SCIENCE?

_____

_____

COMMENTS _____

_____

NAME _____

Discovery Science Family Night: Second Meeting

Dear Family,

As you know, we have incorporated Discovery Science into our school curriculum. The program has been in use for several weeks now, and the children have been doing many of the activities that you were introduced to at our first Discovery Science Family Night. For this second meeting, we want to share what you can do at home to extend this exciting learning experience for your child.

Throughout the year, we will be sending science materials home for your child to share with you. We call these Family Connection activities. Each activity will be enclosed in a resealable plastic bag. The packet will include materials for the activity and instructions as to what you and your child are to do. At this second meeting, we would like you to help us make these packets.

We believe strongly in working hand in hand with families as partners in the education of their children. What better way to do this than an evening where we work together to make science activities from which all of our children and families will benefit?

We want you to be comfortable, so please dress casually. There will be lots of work and fun as we put the Family Connection activities together. There will be something for everyone to do. We will supply the materials, tools, child care, refreshments, and transportation if needed.

We promise there will be no lectures. Please plan to come and share your time and talents with us for the benefit of all the children in our program.

The meeting will be held at _____ on _____ from _____ to _____. If you are able to attend, please return the bottom portion of this letter. Let us know how many adults will be coming and whether you will need child care.

Sincerely,

Please Detach and Return by _____

_____ adults will attend the Discovery Science Family Meeting.

_____ children, ages _____, will need child care.

Transportation needed   Yes   No

We can provide transportation for another family.   Yes   No

Name _____

Phone Number _____

Reminder Flier

DON'T FORGET!

YOU ARE INVITED TO A DISCOVERY SCIENCE FAMILY MEETING

DATE: _____

TIME: _____

PLACE: _____

Come for an evening of fun and socializing while we work together to make science activities your children will share with you at home to promote their discovery of the world of science.

REFRESHMENTS WILL BE SERVED

CHILD CARE WILL BE PROVIDED

Name Tag and Mixer

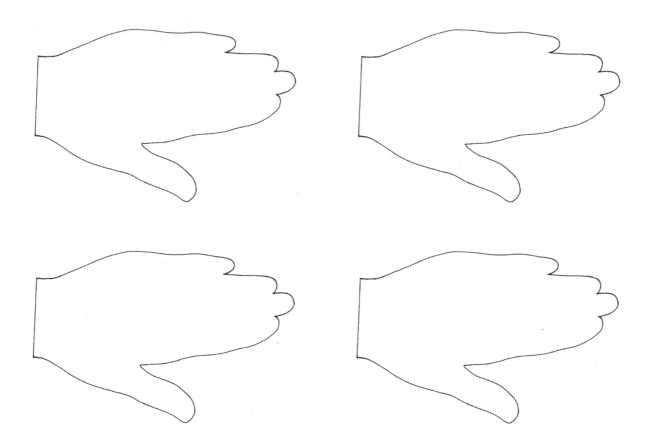

MIXER PROCEDURE

Trace the pattern on colored construction paper. Write a number on the back of each hand (depending on the number of Family Connection activities you will be putting together; if you are constructing all eight activities, you would write one of the numbers 1 through 8 on the back of each name tag). This number will assign each family member to the assembly of one of the Family Connection activities.

As people arrive, hand them a name tag and a pin. Ask that they write their name on the tag, pin it on, and be seated.

When most guests have arrived, have everyone stand in a circle. Give one person a ball of yarn. Say: Please state your name and an activity you enjoy doing at home with your child. After speaking, the person holds the end of the yarn and tosses the ball to another person. The second person states his or her name and an activity, then tosses the ball to a third person while pinching the unraveling strand of yarn at the spot he or she received the ball of yarn. The mixer continues until everyone has had a turn and is pinching a bit of yarn. A web will have been created. Tell the families that the web is symbolic of how we work together to create a positive learning environment for our children. We want them to leave knowing that we need to work together hand in hand as partners for the benefit of their children and to discover that doing science with their children can be an enjoyable experience.

Sample Agenda for Planning the Second Family Night

Purposes: To reinforce the role of families as vital partners in their children's education; to work with families to make Discovery Science Family Connection activities.

Three Weeks Before Meeting

1. Clear meeting date with the center director.
2. Secure authorization for building and room use.
3. Secure a room for child care.
4. Make arrangements for several child-care providers to be on standby; the number needed will depend on the number of children that will be brought.
5. Select a transportation committee chairperson to make arrangements for families who need rides.
6. Select a refreshment committee chairperson. Post a sign-up sheet where families have access to it as they drop off and pick up their children.

Two Weeks Before Meeting

1. Prepare and send invitations.
2. Lay out the physical arrangement of the meeting room on paper.
3. Determine which Family Connection activities will be assembled at the meeting.

One Week Before Meeting

1. Prepare name tags. Prepare evaluation forms and make copies.
2. Collect the materials for the Family Connection activities that are to be assembled at the meeting.
3. Make up sample kits for each of the Family Connection activities to be assembled and write instructions for the assembly of each kit. Indicate how many bags are needed for each Family Connection activity (one per child).
4. Check with the refreshment committee chairperson. Remind families of food they have signed up to bring.
5. Send home a reminder flier with each child.
6. Check with transportation committee chairperson to see if all who need rides can be accommodated.

One Day Before Meeting

1. Send home final reminder.
2. Verify that you have enough child-care providers for the age and number of children coming, and remind child-care providers of the time of the meeting.
3. Check with the transportation committee chairperson to verify rides for families needing them.
4. Check with the refreshment committee chairperson to touch base on arrangements.

Day of Meeting

1. Set up chairs. Set up tables, one for each of the Family Connection activities to be put together.

2. Put up signs directing families to the meeting location.

3. Put name tags, pins, pens or pencils, and Family Connection activities materials in place. Have evaluation forms handy.

Sample Family Meeting Plan

Time	Activity	Technique	Resources/Materials
7:00–7:05	Greeting	Greet people as they arrive. Hand out name tags.	Name tags, pins, pencils or pens
7:05–7:10	Mixer.	Introduce and begin mixer. Stress the value of home/school partnership.	Ball of yarn
7:10–7:20	Introduce Family Connection activities. Explain the procedure to follow during the meeting.	Explain the Family Connection activities while the people are still in the yarn web. Tell them that the number on their name tags indicates the Family Connection activity bag they will assemble. Explain that instructions and a model are at each table.	A copy of *Discovery Science* so people can read the science activity that correlates with the Family Connection activity and understand the relationship between the two.
7:20–7:45	Assemble the Family Connection activity bags.	People go to the tables and assemble the Family Connection activity bags.	Materials to assemble the Family Connection activity bags, one of each per child
7:45–8:00	Reporting	Have the groups from each table choose a spokesperson to explain and demonstrate their completed Family Connection activity and the procedure to be followed when it is brought home.	
8:00–8:30	Closing Evaluation Refreshments	Closing remarks emphasizing the importance of home and school partnership. Discuss care and return procedures for the kits. Hand out evaluation forms. Serve refreshments.	Evaluation forms, pens or pencils

Second Family Meeting Evaluation

EVALUATION

PLEASE CHECK THE HAND THAT BEST DESCRIBES YOUR OPINION
OF TONIGHT'S DISCOVERY SCIENCE MEETING

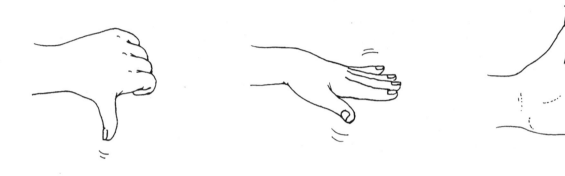

Comments

Will you feel comfortable doing the Family Connection activities at home? Yes No

Would you like more information about the activities? Yes No

If yes, please write your phone number below, and we will contact you:

Name _____

Phone _____

Family Letters and Family Connection Activities

Use these sample letters to write your own family letters announcing each unit. Copy and cut apart the Family Connection activity slips. Send the slips, along with the indicated materials, home with the children at the appropriate times during each unit.

How Objects Are Alike and Different

Dear Family,

Next week your child and I will begin the How Objects Are Alike and Different Unit of Discovery Science. I want to invite you to take part in this experience by becoming involved with our work with *alike* and *different*.

The children will be bringing home some interesting activities to share with you. We call these materials Family Connection activities. Each activity is enclosed in a resealable plastic packet. The packet includes materials for the activity and information about what the children will do. Be prepared to repeat the activity over and over as your child shares the excitement of Discovery Science. Please return the packets in two days with comments from you and your child.

Please remember to let your child show you and tell you what he or she has learned. Letting your child teach you is a great way to make it known that you think what your child is learning is important.

If you have any questions or would like to help in any way, please send a note or call me. Thank you so much for your support and interest in Discovery Science for your child.

Sincerely,

How Objects Are Alike and Different
Family Connection Activity 1

For use with Art Center Activity 3

Crayon Lines

In school we are making long lines of different colors of crayons. Now see how long a line you and your child can make at home with different types of socks. Have you got enough socks to go all the way across the room?

In This Kit You Will Find
directions

You Will Also Need
a collection of socks

What to Do

1. With your child, gather a collection of socks of two different types, such as plain white and striped.

2. Have your child sort the socks into two separate piles by type. Ask which pile seems to have the most socks.

3. Now have your child line up the socks end to end in two lines.

4. Ask your child to tell you which pile made the longest line.

5. You may want to encourage your child to sort the socks by another criteria, such as long and short. You might also want to do this with other things, such as blocks or toys.

How Objects Are Alike and Different
Family Connection Activity 2

For use with Discovery Center Activity 1

Magnets Attract

What does a magnet attract? You and your child might be surprised by some of the objects around the house that are attracted to the magnet.

In This Kit You Will Find
directions
magnet

You Will Also Need
assorted objects, some that are attracted to a magnet and some that aren't

What to Do

1. Walk with your child around the house at see what things you can find that are attracted to the magnet.

2. As your child finds things that are attracted or not attracted to the magnet, have him or her tell you the names so that you can make a list of the discoveries.

3. Send the list to school when you return the kit so your child can share discoveries with the other children.

How Objects Move

Dear Family,

Next week your child and I will begin the How Objects Move Unit of Discovery Science. I want to invite you to take part in this experience by becoming involved with our work with *movement*.

The children will be bringing home some interesting activities to share with you. We call these materials Family Connection activities. Each activity is enclosed in a resealable plastic packet. The packet includes materials for the activity and information about what the children will do. Be prepared to repeat the activity over and over as your child shares the excitement of Discovery Science. Please return the packets in two days with comments from you and your child.

Please remember to let your child show you and tell you what he or she has learned. Letting your child teach you is a great way to make it known that you think what your child is learning is important.

If you have any questions or would like to help in any way, please send a note or call me. Thank you so much for your support and interest in Discovery Science for your child.

Sincerely,

How Objects Move
Family Connection Activity 1

For use with Discovery Center Activity 6

What Rolls?

Today your child collected objects from the classroom and tested their "rollability." Help your child repeat this experience at home. Check the toy shelves, the kitchen cabinets, and under the couch to find things that roll.

In This Kit You Will Find
directions

You Will Also Need
household items, some that roll and some that don't

What to Do

1. Let your child make two collections of items from around the house: one of things they think will roll and one of nonrollers.

2. Help your child test the items. Were they put into the right category? Can some objects be classified in either group depending on how they are rolled?

3. If you wish, you and your child may send me a list of some of the items in each group.

How Objects Move
Family Connection Activity 2

For use with Small Group Activity 1

How Far Can You Jump?

Today we had the children compare the distances they could jump standing still and running. Now you can get your whole family jumping.

In This Kit You Will Find
directions
1-by-3-inch cardboard strips (for marking landing points)

What to Do

1. Have your child show you how far he or she can jump from both a standing start and a running start. Mark the landing points with the cardboard strips.

2. Now it's time for the rest of the family to jump!

3. What did you all find out? If you wish, send the results to school for your child to share with the class.

How Objects Change

Dear Family,

Next week your child and I will begin the How Objects Change Unit of Discovery Science. I want to invite you to take part in this experience by becoming involved with our work with *change*.

The children will be bringing home some interesting activities to share with you. We call these materials Family Connection activities. Each activity is enclosed in a resealable plastic packet. The packet includes materials for the activity and information about what the children will do. Be prepared to repeat the activity over and over as your child shares the excitement of Discovery Science. Please return the packets in two days with comments from you and your child.

Please remember to let your child show you and tell you what he or she has learned. Letting your child teach you is a great way to make it known that you think what your child is learning is important.

If you have any questions or would like to help in any way, please send a note or call me. Thank you so much for your support and interest in Discovery Science for your child.

Sincerely,

How Objects Change
Family Connection Activity 1

For use with Art Center Activity 3

Here Again, Gone Again Colors

Your child has already mixed yellow corn oil and blue food coloring and discovered that the mixture produces green. Now you and your child can discover together what happens when you mix red food coloring with yellow corn oil.

In This Kit You Will Find
directions

You Will Also Need
small jar
yellow corn oil
red food coloring
water

What to Do

1. Fill the jar with half corn oil and half water. Add a couple drops of red food coloring. Have your child tell you what he or she sees.

2. Let your child shake the jar and describe what he or she sees. What happens when he or she stops shaking the jar?

3. If you wish, write down your child's observations to bring to school when returning the kit.

How Objects Change
Family Connection Activity 2

For use with Discovery Center Activity 1

Water into Ice, Isn't That Nice?

Today the children made ice cubes to water plants. Now let them make fruit juice cubes to "water" themselves and their family.

In This Kit You Will Find
directions

You Will Also Need
fruit juice
5 to 10 three-ounce paper cups
5 to 10 craft sticks

What to Do

1. Let your child fill the cups with juice of his or her choice.

2. Have your child place a craft stick in each cup.

3. Place the cups in the freezer.

4. When the juice has frozen, your child may remove the cups from the freezer and quench everybody's thirst.

How Objects Are Made and Used

Dear Family,

Next week your child and I will begin the How Objects Are Made and Used Unit of Discovery Science. I want to invite you to take part in this experience by becoming involved with our work with *technology* and *tools*.

The children will be bringing home some interesting activities to share with you. We call these materials Family Connection activities. Each activity is enclosed in a resealable plastic packet. The packet includes materials for the activity and information about what the children will do. Be prepared to repeat the activity over and over as your child shares the excitement of Discovery Science. Please return the packets in two days with comments from you and your child.

Please remember to let your child show you and tell you what he or she has learned. Letting your child teach you is a great way to make it known that you think what your child is learning is important.

If you have any questions or would like to help in any way, please send a note or call me. Thank you so much for your support and interest in Discovery Science for your child.

Sincerely,

How Objects Are Made and Used
Family Connection Activity 1

For use with Block Center Activity 4

Ramps

This activity can be a lot of fun! Try to find the fastest downhill rollers in your home.

In This Kit You Will Find
directions

You Will Also Need
game board
cookie sheet or other item to use as a ramp
books or blocks
objects that will roll, such as balls and pencils

What to Do

1. Let your child show you how to make a ramp using the board and blocks or books.

2. Help your child find things to roll down the ramp.

3. Encourage your child to guess which objects will roll the fastest, then test out the predictions.

4. If you wish, you may send me a list of the items your child thinks are the best rollers. We'll talk about this at school and see what everyone discovered.

5. Your child may want to bring one of the fastest rollers to school to share with the other children.

How Objects Are Made and Used
Family Connection Activity 2

For use with Discovery Center Activity 4

Help Me Pick These Up

We have been using a variety of tools to pick up and move objects. Now let's see what you have at home that can do the same task.

In This Kit You Will Find
directions

You Will Also Need
tools that will pick things up
items to pick up

What to Do

1. Go with your child on a hunt around the house to find things that will pick up small items, such as tweezers, tongs, pliers, and chopsticks. Try to find at least two "picker-uppers."

2. Now collect some small items to be picked up, such as cotton balls, acorns, small toys, and bolts.

3. Watch your child test the tools. Encourage your child to try a variety of combinations. For example, tongs will pick up a toy car. Will tweezers?

Other Educational Materials in This Series

Available in 1996:
Discovery Science for Grades 1 Through 3

Other Innovative Learning Publications™ Books Relating to Early Childhood Science

For more information or to order call, (800) 552-2259.